Take It From ME

An Insider's Guide to Maine Restaurants, Inns, and Lodges

George and Linda Smith

The Travelin' Maine(rs)

ISLANDPORT PRESS

Islandport Press
P.O. Box 10
247 Portland Street
Yarmouth, Maine 04096
www.islandportpress.com
info@islandportpress.com

ISBN: 978-1-939017-84-0
Library of Congress Card Number: 2015945272

Dean L. Lunt, publisher

TABLE OF CONTENTS

Linda Smith at the Spruce Point Inn in Boothbay Harbor.

Introduction: He Said, She Said

When Mainers like us go on vacation, we often go to . . .
Maine. We know the best places, and look forward to visiting
them often. These are not always places you have heard or
read about. We have some real gems in Maine, and oftentimes
we Mainers like to keep them secret. Well, we're going to spill
some of those secrets.

Linda and I have traveled the world during our forty years
together, but our favorite vacation spots, inns, and restaurants are all right here in our home state. (Okay, there is that
wonderful little apartment we love in Greve, Italy, and that
small house we rent in Terlingua, Texas, but this book is about
Maine!)

At the end of 2010, when I retired from the Sportsman's
Alliance of Maine to write full-time, I wanted something Linda
(a retired first-grade teacher) and I could do together. Given
our love for travel, a travel column seemed like a good idea.

Our local daily newspapers, the *Kennebec Journal* and the
Morning Sentinel, embraced the idea, and we began writing a
weekly travel column.

We are now in our sixth year as The Travelin' Maine(rs),
as we are known in the newspaper, and enjoy alerting readers
to our favorite places, events, and activities in our beautiful
state. Many folks have asked when we were going to write a
book. Well, here it is! This book reveals our favorite places in
Maine—the ones to put on your travel bucket list. We've organized them to fit your schedule and travel interests: Twenty-
Four-Hour (or Longer) Getaways; Special Places for Special
Celebrations; and Don't-Miss Restaurants.

Linda and I both offer our own opinions on each place
we visit. Linda is the real food expert. She's a great cook and
a year-round gardener, with a fourteen-by-twenty-eight-foot
hoop house that produces greens all winter long.

For many travelers, it's all about expectations. The best places want to meet yours, so we'll tell you what you can expect at each destination. We look for value, comfort, creativity, and great service—always important to us, and we're sure it's important to you, too. We often find that the owners and chefs come with compelling stories of their own, and we love to tell those stories. It's been a real treat getting to know so many wonderful people in the course of our travels.

You won't find just the best-known places in this book—although we've included a few, because they are among our favorites. Instead, we focus on the lesser-known, surprisingly wonderful places that Linda and I have discovered all over the state, as well as those that were already our favorites long before we began the travel column—the ones that usually make Linda exclaim, when leaving, "Oh, I want to come back here!"

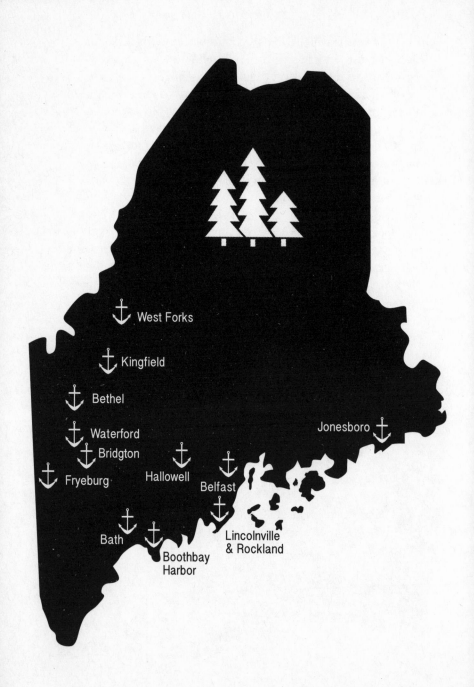

West Forks

Kingfield

Bethel

Waterford

Bridgton

Jonesboro

Fryeburg

Hallowell

Belfast

Bath

Lincolnville
& Rockland

Boothbay
Harbor

Getaways
Twenty-Four-Hour (or Longer)

Bath	The Inn at Bath
Belfast	Fireside Inn & Suites Ocean's Edge
Bethel	The Bethel Inn Resort
Boothbay Harbor	Tugboat Inn and Fisherman's Wharf Inn
Bridgton	Noble House Inn
Fryeburg	The Oxford House Inn
Fryeburg	The Stone Mountain Arts Center and The Old Saco Inn
Hallowell	Maple Hill Farm Bed & Breakfast
Jonesboro	Chandler River Lodge
Kingfield	One Stanley Avenue Restaurant and Three Stanley Avenue Bed & Breakfast
Lincolnville	The Youngtown Inn and Restaurant
Rockland	Berry Manor Inn
Rockland	LimeRock Inn
Waterford	Waterford Inne and Restaurant
West Forks	Northern Outdoors Adventure Resort

The Getaways

You can enjoy a wonderful time at these places in just twenty-four hours. But these are also places where you can linger for days, exploring the region and returning each night to your comfortable room.

Many of our favorite inns also have restaurants, and each restaurant listed here is remarkable. So even if you are not able to stay at these inns, put their restaurants on your culinary bucket list.

In many of our columns, we enjoy telling the stories of the owners, innkeepers, and chefs. Their inns and restaurants are their lives. They are on duty 24/7, able to handle the guests who become longtime friends, as well as the customers from hell. We actually enjoy hearing about the latter.

Prices and hours of operation can change frequently, so we have not included them in the reviews in this book. Also, some places may close during the winter months. We have listed website addresses and telephone numbers and we encourage you use them to learn more information before planning to visit any of the places listed. We also encourage you to make reservations whenever possible, which can often make your travel experience more enjoyable.

Bath
The Inn at Bath

969 Washington Street, Bath
(800) 423-0964, (207) 443-4294
www.innatbath.com

Minutes from *PORTLAND: 40, BANGOR: 105*

Who knew that Bath was a vacation destination? After years of driving by this community—a place where Mainers have built ships for so many years, and still do, at Bath Iron Works (BIW)—we stopped for a night at The Inn at Bath. We met others there on weekend getaways from Chelsea, Maine, to Chicago, Illinois. And because of a snowstorm, our stop turned into a very enjoyable three-day visit.

Our search for interesting cities and towns in Maine led us to Bath. We were already familiar with our state's prominent shipbuilder, BIW, as well as, nearby Reid State Park and Popham Beach. But I was pleasantly surprised by how much is going on in the downtown section of the city. A variety of local shops caught my eye, including the Cooking Emporium and the Mariner's Compass quilting shop. There are many restaurants and art galleries, along with a health-food store and so much more.

We crammed a lot into our visit—the Winter Wonderland Art Exhibit and a play at the **Chocolate Church Arts Center**, a Saturday-night concert at the **Winter Street Center** (another former church), a fine dinner at **Solo Bistro**, and a fascinating visit to the **Maine Maritime Museum**.

Our stay at **The Inn at Bath** was certainly a highlight of our getaway. Located in one of the large historic houses on

Washington Street, this year-round bed-and-breakfast was an ideal location within easy walking distance of downtown. The fact that it was a snowy weekend made it even more delightful. Walking around in light snow gave us the full winter experience in a small New England town.

As you enter this inn you will find a packet on the counter with your name on it and a gold key ring with a large gold jingle bell on it. You won't misplace this key! The stunning dining room alerts you that breakfast is a priority here. The table is set, complete with a vase of fresh tulips in beautiful pastel colors. Two sitting rooms are so cozy that guests are drawn in to enjoy the fire and conversation. One thing I love about staying in an historic inn is the chance to appreciate old homes with interesting architectural designs.

Innkeeper Elizabeth Knowlton has tastefully decorated her inn with artwork featuring flowers and birds that blends with the comfortable furniture in a most inviting way. She must also have a green thumb, because there are orchids and even a tree with small oranges on it in the dining room. You will want to linger here.

The inn was full our first night, which gave us an opportunity to meet an array of interesting people at breakfast. One couple was from Chelsea, Maine (the husband wanted to treat his schoolteacher wife to a short getaway). Another couple came from Ithaca, New York, to see their daughter (a freshman at Amherst) compete in a swim meet at Bowdoin College. And we had wonderful conversations with a couple from Chicago, who were enjoying a long weekend with their son and his girlfriend, who live in Massachusetts.

The Winter Wonderland Art Exhibit at the Chocolate Church was beautiful, featuring eight artists and pieces focused on nature in winter. I loved the gorgeous photographs of Joan Cyr and Rob Smith, and Leon Vanella's black-and-white photographs printed on metal. The 3-D paintings featuring birch stands with crows and red berries by Karen Dominguez were my favorite, but I also loved the encaustic hot-wax paintings of Jane Page-Conway. It was an amazing variety of mediums in one show.

Although it turned windy and the snow continued to fall on Saturday night, I loved the beauty of it all, safely watching from our second-floor windows. On Sunday, as the wind gusted up to fifty miles an hour and snow piled up in the streets, we decided this was a great place to stay and watch it all happen. We signed up to stay another night, making our way to the city's eating places on foot. It's an adventure I'll remember.

Innkeeper Elizabeth Knowlton has clearly created a home away from home for travelers at her Inn at Bath, but Mainers have also discovered this elegant and comfortable inn. I was impressed that the couple from Chicago selected this inn after an extensive online search—including a telephone conversation with Elizabeth—before they reserved their room.

Highlights for me were our beautiful room with a gorgeous canopied bed, two community rooms downstairs for sitting, reading, and visiting with newly made friends, the downstairs fireplace, where I warmed myself each time we returned from a cold walk, and the large gathering table in the dining room, where we could breakfast and converse with other guests.

Elizabeth's breakfasts deserve special mention. Oatmeal, fresh fruit, yogurt, granola, juices, and coffee are always served, along with a hot dish. These are cloth-napkin, heavy-cutlery, fresh-flower, fine-dining breakfasts. The first morning she served a tasty French toast of pumpkin bread, plus sausages on the side. The second morning we were blessed with a perfectly poached egg served with bacon, lettuce, and tomato on toasted bread. The bacon was thick and crispy, the tomatoes were grown in Madison, Maine. We lingered for half an hour after eating, visiting with Elizabeth and her guests—two of whom came up from Boston to bird-watch on a wintry Reid State Park beach. Brrr!

I especially loved visiting with Elizabeth, a world traveler who once owned and cooked at a Montana fly-fishing lodge. You can guess what we talked about! From Montana to Alaska, we swapped fishing stories.

Our favorite inns always feature a wonderful host, and Elizabeth is certainly that. We left the inn on Monday morning after enjoying a delightful stay, discovering another great Maine destination, and making a bunch of new friends.

Belfast
Fireside Inn & Suites Ocean's Edge

159 Searsport Avenue, Belfast
(207) 338-2090
www.belfastmainehotel.com

Ocean's Edge Restaurant
(207) 338-2646

Cuisine *AMERICAN* | Minutes from *PORTLAND: 120, BANGOR: 50*

Belfast is filled with wonderful art galleries and gift shops, an awesome co-op, nice lodgings and delicious food—all right by the ocean. Belfast is one of our favorite coastal towns for a weekend getaway.

 On a sunny (practically balmy) day in February, we strolled the main street of Belfast, popping in to visit a variety of businesses. The previous night's snow was melting into slushy goop on the corners of the intersections. I found myself taking special pleasure in tromping right through the messiness, which brought back satisfying memories of those same spring delights when I was a kid.

You could see it on people's faces: We were going to make it through this interminably long winter. In the same vein, visiting two of my favorite places in Belfast made me even happier. I fell in love with the **Belfast Co-op** on my previous visit. This charming co-op is the largest and one of the oldest in Maine, with a strong commitment to Maine products. They sold $1.67 Million worth of Maine products last year.

One can find an array of organic, ethnic, and hard-to-find ingredients at the co-op. I spend most of my time in the bulk-food aisle. I measured and weighed my way through oat flour, pearl couscous, sesame sticks, yellow split peas, soba noodles, and sesame seeds. I looked longingly at the great selection of house-made sausages and choices from the dairy cooler. But we were staying another day, so it wasn't practical to purchase things that needed immediate refrigeration.

The co-op has 3,500 members, and I would certainly join their ranks if I lived closer, but the prices here are reasonable regardless of membership.

George had heard great things about a brewery and restaurant on the water. We discovered that they aren't open for lunch, just dinner, and though George was a bit disappointed, I smiled, knowing that I would get a chance to go back to **Chase's Daily,** another of my favorite eateries in Belfast. The aroma of freshly baked breads and pastries hits you when you enter. Chase's is my idea of the perfect lunch spot.

We decided to split a bowl of potato leek soup, the soup of the day. Theirs was a sophisticated version served with char-grilled toast. All other versions of this dish I've tried have been cream-based, but this one featured a vegetarian broth packed with flavor. Whoa!

One whiff and a quick glimpse of the pizza arriving at the next table had us quickly abandoning our plan for vegetarian versions of a Reuben and banh mi sandwiches. We went with the margarita pizza—a simple fresh basil, tomato, and mozzarella version. The crust was thin, foldable, and extra crunchy on the bottom. Absolutely awesome. We split the ten-inch size, a perfect amount with our soup starter. At the shop located inside the restaurant, I drooled over the variety of reasonably priced breads.

We dined at the Fireside Inn's Ocean's Edge Restaurant the first night we arrived in Belfast. We were guests at the inn and lucked out by having our dinner reservation there that night. We were in the middle of quite a snowstorm, and I heard several diners say they had given up trying to reach their destinations. They were happy to stay here and watch the snow coming down through windows that overlook the well-lit patio.

I began my meal with the Chef's Seasonal Bliss Salad. This was a nice combination of apples, walnuts, figs, and gorgonzola. Mmmm!

There is a wide variety on this menu. You can choose from hand-tossed pizzas, lots of seafood, or one of their amazing home-style dinners.

But it was on the specials menu that I found a deliciously different dish—chicken breast stuffed with goat cheese and prosciutto. To start with, it had three of my favorite ingredients. The seasoning for the coating added flavor and kept the chicken very moist. It was served with a balsamic reduction with a hint of sweetness, which paired well with the goat cheese and prosciutto. The chef created this special, so I hope he insists that it becomes a regular entree on the menu. It's a winner!

I guess you can tell that Linda loves the Belfast Co-op. But she didn't mention the beer selection or the tasty pastries and sandwiches in the co-op's café.

I agree that Chase's Daily is a great restaurant. The pizza was special. I was thinking I could have eaten an entire pizza, when Linda said, "I'm glad we didn't each get our own pizza!" Ah, well.

We enjoyed dinner at the Ocean's Edge Restaurant, part of the Fireside Inn on Route One, the place that has become our home away from home in Belfast. Our room had an ocean view, a fireplace, and a massage chair. The massage was certainly nice after a long day of walking up and down the steep streets of Belfast.

The Ocean's Edge Restaurant is elegant—lots of wood, a large fireplace with a crackling fire, and huge windows with an ocean view. We took a table near the fireplace and settled in for the evening. Our server Samantha was knowledgeable and did not hurry us through the meal.

Carol, the food manager who was also taking care of things at the inn that weekend, was a superb host, and said they'd been busy this winter. Many Mainers stay here, from contestants at Belfast's curling tournaments to traveling businesspeople and folks looking for a winter escape.

I started with an appetizer they had just added to the menu: a rich cheddar-cheese fondue with spicy chorizo sausage, served with thick slices of French bread. Much to Lin's dismay, I ate all of it. At one point she said, "Don't feel you have to eat all that cheese. It's your weekly allotment."

After watching huge snowflakes dropping out of the sky and feeling pretty good about our spot near the fire, I turned my attention to an extensive list of entrees. The baked stuffed haddock called my name—Atlantic haddock with house-made crabmeat stuffing, topped with a white wine cream sauce and a sprinkle of Parmesan cheese, baked initially and finished under the broiler. And yes, it was every bit as good as it sounds. The portion was huge, and the first bite, heavenly.

I couldn't eat it all (probably that darned cheese filled me up!), but Linda was worse. When she stopped eating her entree, it didn't look like she'd even started. Thank goodness we had a small fridge in our room for leftovers.

But the best was yet to come. We took a delicious chocolate dessert to our room, started the fire, and enjoyed the dessert while watching television. My idea of an evening out!

The inn provides a nice hot breakfast (and you can enjoy it in your slippers), but we didn't stick around long because a major storm was blowing in. The ride home was long and treacherous. It all made me wish we had stayed another day!

Bethel
The Bethel Inn Resort

21 Broad Street, Bethel
(800) 654-0125
www.bethelinn.com

Minutes from *PORTLAND: 95, BANGOR: 150*

There is a lot to celebrate and enjoy in Bethel, which seems to have a special event every weekend. It's a busy place, partly because of the nearby Sunday River ski area. This large, multi-building historic inn is a destination, hosting weddings and other events.

Western Maine is a beautiful area, and Bethel is one of our favorite towns. We've visited during peak fall foliage, and cross-country-skied here in the winter. We've come for their Harvest Fest celebration on the town common, and George loves to fish the river and ponds in this area. In fact, while I judged pies at Harvest Fest, he competed in a fishing contest. Bethel is a four-season destination, and the town capitalizes on this fact, offering events and activities throughout the year.

The first time I saw the Bethel Inn I was impressed at its size and surrounding buildings. Built in 1913 and adorned with classic yellow paint, the main building has been kept in good shape. Suites we have stayed in are spacious and comfortable. Our most recent "superior" room included a kitchenette complete with dishes, glasses, silverware, coffeemaker, refrigerator, and microwave. The sleeping and sitting areas were separated, but a flat-screen TV pulled out so that you could turn it to face whichever area you were sitting in. A couch and chairs invited lounging.

Two common rooms downstairs offer ample space for relaxing by the fire, playing a game or enjoying some quiet reading time. Large rooms for events and meetings are available, and they have a conference center across the street.

The inn has 158 rooms located in the main building and one of the separate buildings, and they also offer town houses. From traditional rooms and suites to one-, two-, or three-bedroom luxury town houses and condominiums, you are sure to find something to meet your needs, whether it is a reunion, retreat, wedding, golf outing, or ski adventure.

A buffet is served in the main dining room each morning. Dinners are served in this dining room on Friday and Saturday evenings and during holiday weeks. **The Millbrook Tavern and Grill** located downstairs serves traditional pub fare for lunch and dinner, seven days a week.

The Bethel Inn is six miles from Sunday River, and close to New Hampshire's White Mountains. Take a drive and enjoy the beauty!

Bethel is always busy, a place where Mainers and tourists alike gather to enjoy a steady schedule of events. During one visit, I spent Saturday morning at a fly-fishing expo in the Bethel Inn's conference facility. Fun! And boy, did that event whet my appetite for the open-water fishing season.

The inn is historic. It started out catering to "outpatients" whose therapy included psychiatric treatment and a physical workout. Owner Scott Davis purchased the inn in 2008 and upgraded the food and facilities. The year-round outdoor pool is popular, and I have enjoyed several exceptional meals in the tavern. If you are lucky enough to be there on Mexican Night, don't miss the Rattlesnake Bites. While you might expect great meat dishes (the rack of ribs is my favorite), I have been especially impressed with their seafood.

I was at the inn in June of 2013 during its hundredth anniversary celebration, attending a conference for travel and outdoor writers. We crammed in a lot of activities over three days. I was particularly taken by a presentation from the local historical society, which has an impressive museum just down the street from the inn.

On one trip here, we took a scenic ride through the mountains, up and over Evans Notch on Route 113 from Gilead to Fryeburg. We enjoyed a picnic at a scenic stop at Basin Pond along the way, with a lunch we purchased at **The Good Food Store** on Route 2 in Bethel—a little place packed with good stuff, from wine to sweet potatoes.

There is so much to do in the general area, but also a lot to keep you right on the grounds of the Bethel Inn, including a terrific golf course and, in the winter, a cross-country ski trail. The inn's health club, in addition to the outside pool, has saunas, a Jacuzzi, a fitness room, and massage treatments. There is live weekend entertainment in the tavern. We also saw quite a few people taking advantage of the Mountain Explorer ski shuttle to Sunday River that picks you up right at the inn.

It's all good, including the Bethel Inn's rooms and food, and the area's events and conferences will keep you coming back on a regular basis. These folks know how to do tourism right.

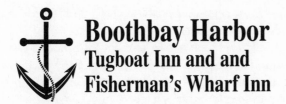

Boothbay Harbor
Tugboat Inn and and Fisherman's Wharf Inn

Tugboat Inn
80 Commercial Street
(800) 248-2628, (207) 633-4434
www.tugboatinn.com

Fisherman's Wharf Inn
Pier 6, 22 Commercial Street
(800) 628-6872, (207) 633-5090
www.fishermanswharfinn.com

Cuisine *AMERICAN* | Minutes from *PORTLAND: 75, BANGOR: 125*

A rainy Memorial Day weekend didn't dampen our spirits, probably because we had a comfortable room right on the harbor, three great restaurants to try, a host of shops and galleries to explore, and some great local places to bird-watch.

 The Tugboat Inn has clean, beautiful rooms looking directly out onto the harbor. Our corner room gave way to the water in each direction. This is a charming harbor lined with hotels and restaurants, all within easy walking distance of downtown shopping. The inn has sixty-two rooms in five separate buildings.

The rooms are large and include a sitting area. Amenities include a refrigerator, Keurig coffeemaker, two bureaus, flat-screen TV, and a balcony. The king-size bed loaded with pillows was comfortable.

Even on a drizzly day the view from the rooms is charming. Boats are docked at the wharves and throughout the harbor.

From the Tugboat Inn you can look straight across the harbor to the inns and restaurants on Atlantic Avenue.

The first night we ate dinner at the Tugboat Restaurant. The open dining room provides spectacular views of the harbor.

I knew I wanted crab cakes as soon as I saw the menu. The appetizer consisted of two crab cakes, George suggested we share an order, but I held fast to ordering my own. Good thing, as these were far too delicious to only have one. Served with microgreens and a chipotle aioli, the crab cakes were everything I had hoped for, and then some. They were crunchy on the outside with a seasoned crust, and moist and tender crabmeat on the inside.

I don't eat much seafood, but I do enjoy both crabmeat and Maine shrimp. Hoping that a fried Maine shrimp dinner wouldn't be heavy, I chose that. How they made the batter so light and kept the shrimp greaseless, I'll never know. Instead of a little cup of tartar sauce, they brought large bottles of tartar sauce and cocktail sauce to our table. This meal left no room for dessert.

Lunch at Fisherman's Wharf was great fun. We ate in the lounge and declared it the perfect day for soup and more crabmeat. My cup of cream of vegetable soup with chicken and cheddar was memorable. It was piping hot, creamy, and full of flavor. The crab cakes featured different seasonings than those I'd had the night before and I really enjoyed the mango salsa served with them.

The meal was enhanced by mellow music performed by Curt Bessette and Jenn Kurtz from Eliot, Maine. They were so good, singing tunes we knew, that we lingered well into the afternoon.

It was a drizzly Saturday, and I all but had to drag George out birding in the morning. After reading of a birding hot spot at the **Boothbay Region Land Trust's Lobster Cove Preserve** in Bob Duchesne's Maine Birding Trail book, I was insistent. The well-marked trails are wonderful places to walk even if you are not a bird-watcher. The trails take you through woods, fields, and along a water-filled bog. We found lots of birds in a set of apple trees and along the water. George later admitted he was very glad we went.

Lafayette Hotels does hospitality right. The family owns several hotels in Maine and New Hampshire. In Boothbay Harbor, they own three: the Boothbay Harbor Inn, Fisherman's Wharf Inn, and Tugboat Inn. On this visit, we were staying the Tugboat Inn and we ate at the inn's restaurant on the night we arrived.

It's nice to find a restaurant that features Maine wine and beer. The Tugboat offered wine from **Cellardoor Winery** in Lincolnville and beers brewed by Shipyard, Geary's, and Marshall's Wharf.

I suggested we begin by sharing an appetizer of crab cakes, only to hear, "I'm not sharing my crab cakes with you!" Well, that still worked worked out okay because we both ordered the crabcake appetizer and as a result I got a full order to myself. We've been building a list of the best crab cakes in Maine over the past two years, and these went immediately into the top five. Even the presentation was great, with the chipotle sauce cleverly hidden inside a radicchio leaf.

Ann, our server, worked here for more than twenty years. She left for a few years to work in real estate, but then returned when the recession hit. Now she serves here in season, but also continues to sell real estate—a typical Mainer with more than one job. She's a keeper, and she kept us both entertained and well fed throughout the evening.

We enjoyed watching and listening to Ann serve a nearby table of tourists, most of whom ordered lobster in the shell. One of them totally shredded her bib trying to put it on, and Ann was quick to joke, "That's okay. It's only a six-dollar charge for another bib!" And when she brought the lady a new bib, Ann put it on for her. Not taking another chance on that!

I had settled on seafood pie as my entree, until Ann told us the specials. Halibut topped with fresh crabmeat and hollandaise sauce hit three of my favorites all in one dish. It came with tasty rice that included onions and corn.

All of this consumed two hours, at a table that afforded a view of the harbor and, about a mile out, Burnt Island, owned by the public and managed by our Bureau of Parks and Lands. If you've never been there, put it on your bucket list. Several charters in Boothbay Harbor will take you there—or you can kayak out to it, as we have done a number of times.

The history of each of the Tugboat Inn's five buildings fascinated me. At one time they housed everything from a chandlery to the **Boothbay Harbor Yacht Club**. The Tugboat itself (and yes, there is one) was built in 1917 and worked all along the New England coast before coming to roost here, where it now houses a restaurant and lounge.

Inn manager Bonnie Stover is a great host, and we're already eager to return—next time, on a hot, sunny weekend!

Bridgton
Noble House Inn

81 Highland Road, Bridgton
(888) 237-4880, (207) 647-3733
www.noblehousebb.com

Cuisine *ITALIAN* | Minutes from *PORTLAND: 70, BANGOR: 150*

The Noble House Inn is located in the heart of western Maine, offering nearby skiing, shopping, lakes, hiking trails, and the Fryeburg Fair. And, oh yeah, a terrific restaurant, too!

 While staying at the Noble House Inn, I turned my wicker chair around to enjoy the snow-covered maple tree right outside our second-story window, with the tall pine forest beyond, along with my morning coffee.

I also do this at home—turn my rocking chair around to look out our large kitchen window while enjoying my coffee and the *Kennebec Journal* every morning. But at the inn, I was missing the chickadees that crowd the bird feeder right outside our kitchen window—until I looked at my coffee cup. It featured a painting of a chickadee!

The thoughtfulness poured into every room of the Noble House Inn is amazing. And innkeeper Cindi Hooper is a vivacious, super-friendly host. Cindi was a high-powered attorney in her native Texas when she decided a career change was in order.

Her personal story is interesting. In summary, she visited in 1999 to bury her mother's ashes in the South Bridgton/ Adams Pond cemetery. Not surprisingly, Cindi fell in love with our state. Eventually, she found a way to return and live here.

Ever since we first visited The Noble House Inn in 2011, we looked forward to getting back and enjoying it place again. We finally did and it was just as good on the return trip. We even asked Cindi if she would change the name of our second-floor room, the Noble Suite, to The Travelin' Maine(rs) Suite!

Cindi has embraced the greater Bridgton community and enthusiastically recommends many local shops and restaurants, including the **Black Horse Tavern**, where we enjoyed a great dinner.The Noble House Inn itself hosts many weddings, musical events, and special dinners during the holidays.

Bridgton's business district was shining bright with Christmas lights and featured everything a visitor might need, from a great bookstore, **Bridgton Books** to art, crafts, and wine shops, restaurants and pubs, and the largest **Renys** we had ever seen.

We ate breakfast at the Inn. It alternates savory and sweet breakfasts, and, of course, Linda and I couldn't agree on which we wanted, so Cindi cooked a savory breakfast for Linda and a sweet one for me. Yes, we are spoiled!

My pecan-crusted French toast was so deliciously sweet that I didn't use any maple syrup. The candied bacon was something I had never had but will dream about from now on. And I even loved my taste of the green beans and cheese included on Linda's plate. When I asked about the cheese, Cindi whipped out a brochure for the nearby **Old School Creamery**. She really does love to promote local businesses.

"It's a magical place. I feel like I'm just the caretaker," Cindi said of her bed-and-breakfast.

I love the story of her arrival at the inn, the day after purchasing it. It took her two and a half hours to drive from Gorham to Bridgton in a blizzard, and she had four hundred items to unload. In the midst of that chore, she looked down the driveway and the couple next door was walking up with a welcoming card, coffee, and food. No wonder she loves Maine!

Entering Bridgton's Noble House Inn during any time of year is impressive, but one step inside during the Christmas season is sure to please your senses. The tasteful decorations are subtle here—a small tree of silver and white in the parlor window, Christmas mugs and tableware, and sprinkles of Christmas accents throughout the house.

The Noble House is comfortably elegant. The fire is going in the fireplace, and you can help yourself to hot or cold drinks to go with Cindi's homemade cookies in the jar. One of the best things about staying at a B&B is that it feels intimate. As Cindi gave us an introductory tour, it was clear that she wants guests to make themselves at home. Lots of reading material is available, the selection of music and DVDs is vast, and there is a closet full of games and puzzles. George even found mystery novels by his favorite authors in our room. (Later, Cindi told us she arrived from Texas with thirty-six cartons of books!)

We stayed in the Noble Suite, a beautiful space located on the second floor. The main room features many windows, a four-poster bed, an armoire, and a vaulted ceiling. I quickly noted the fresh pale-pink tulips in the bay window next to a martini glass filled with chocolates. The suite includes a sitting room with a love seat and TV, and a large bathroom with a Jacuzzi tub. Robes with the Noble House insignia hang invitingly nearby.

The king-size bed and selection of pillows provided a great night's sleep, and we awoke to a winter wonderland. This room is located close to the wooded side of the property, and all the trees had a coating of new snow.

The breakfast table was set with Christmas in mind, and flowers were placed at each table. Oatmeal was available, with a variety of toppings, and Cindi brought juice and a fruit starter.

I'd never heard of vanilla brûlée grapefruit before, but I will tell you that it was amazing. Breaking through the crusty topping, a thin layer of crème brûlée rested on the sectioned fruit. You wouldn't think that grapefruit could combine with dairy, but believe me, it did.

My breakfast plate was quiche Lorraine, a strip of candied bacon, and green beans with a dollop of locally made lemon goat cheese. The quiche had a flaky crust with a creamy filling, and the green beans were super. I loved the candied bacon due to her addition of cracked pepper, making it both savory and sweet.

Snow continued to drift down throughout our breakfast as we enjoyed a leisurely start to our day and lovely conversation with Cindi. She mentioned her love of the four seasons as one of the reasons she chose the Bridgton area to settle. Some people do not like winter snows, but I find a new snowfall incredibly beautiful, and I could see that Cindi appreciated the scene as well.

Do come and visit the Noble House Inn, no matter what the season. You will be welcome and you will eat well.

Fryeburg
The Oxford House Inn

548 Main Street, Fryeburg
(800) 261-7206, (207) 935-3442
www.oxfordhouseinn.com

Cuisine *AMERICAN* | Minutes from *PORTLAND: 75, BANGOR: 165*

What do you get when you combine a stunning view of Maine's western mountains, a historic, lovingly restored inn, and delicious, creative cuisine? You get Fryeburg's The Oxford House Inn.

We needed help to discover the Oxford House Inn. There aren't a lot of places to stay in the Fryeburg-Brownfield, but we absolutely love the **Stone Mountain Arts Center** and its musical performances. So, we asked Stone Mountain's owner,

Carol Noonan, for a few recommendations. She was effusive in her praise of the Oxford House Inn for both lodging and food.

Carol did not overstate the case. Jonathon and Natalie Spak are friendly hosts, and we felt at home from the moment Natalie greeted us upon arrival.

The house was designed and built in 1913 by John Calvin Stevens for the Fox family on the site of an old hotel. The exposed granite walls downstairs remain from the hundred-room hotel that burned in 1906. When the Spaks arrived in 2007, the inn was serving as a doctor's office. Some rooms were closed off. They tore the building apart, discovered beautiful original-wood walls and other special features, and then restored it.

The back dining room overlooks Weston's Farm and the mountains beyond. We claimed a table there for dinner and breakfast the following day, captivated by the view. I imagine the Adirondack chairs and fire pit on the back lawn are popular on summer evenings as guests enjoy stunning sunsets and s'mores.

The inn gets much of its fresh produce from **Weston's Farm and Market**. (Weston's is the farm that grows the potatoes used to make Cold River vodka an international hit.) Guests at the inn can put together a picnic and walk through the Weston's Farm fields to a private beach on the nearby Saco River—yet another reason to schedule a summer visit here.

We do recommend making a reservation well ahead of time, as the inn has just four guest rooms. But even if you can't get a room here, the large restaurant, with three first-floor rooms and a downstairs bar, gives you an opportunity to enjoy very fine dining when you're in the area and North Conway, New Hampshire, with its extensive shopping is just twelve minutes from the inn.

Jonathon Spak is the chef, and his creativity is impressive. My dinner was unforgettable, starting with Crispy Four-Cheese Stuffed Risotto Croquettes—served with warm tomato jam. When I spotted fresh halibut on the menu—my favorite fish—I looked no further for an entree. The large portions of halibut—crispy outside and moist inside—were paired with pieces of lobster, accompanied by an escarole and crispy corn polenta. The halibut was topped with porcini dust. Every bite was like opening a present stuffed with surprises. First, a forkful of halibut, then a bit of escarole or leeks, then add some lobster or polenta—wow!

You will find all this amazing, but even after all this food, I still had room for Irish Coffee Cream Puffs—Bailey's Irish Cream mascarpone, espresso hot fudge, and caramel sauce.

As soon as you step into the Oxford House Inn you will notice its luxury. A beautiful reception area provides comfortable seating for conversation or reading. Large beams and dark cypress woodwork are featured in the dining rooms, set off with painted walls in a muted teal color. A spiral staircase leads to the four guest rooms upstairs.

Our room was tastefully decorated. Antique picture-fabric adorns the headboard and valances. A granite-topped sink sits in an old cabinet. Two comfortable chairs provide a place to enjoy your morning coffee while enjoying a stunning view.

Oh, and there's a gourmet restaurant on the first floor. The Oxford House has three dining rooms and a small bar. Two feel more formal, with the dark woodwork and beautiful lighting. The one with the porch-like feel overlooking the mountains of New Hampshire is where you should sit if you arrive to dine before dark. The view is peaceful, with large cornfields (birds swooping here and there) nearby and mountains looming in the distance. A labeled drawing helps guests figure out the names of the mountains.

The fresh flowers and white tablecloths on the table are inviting. Soon after you sit, warm homemade focaccia bread arrives. Pleasant music plays in the background, soft enough to allow conversation. You will not want to rush through a meal here, as the view is breathtaking—and the food, too!

My appetizer was a roasted pear and cambozola cheese tart. Caramelized onions and pine nuts, a little arugula, and served in crust. Whoa! So good.

I am always drawn to homemade pasta, and theirs was a basil fettuccine. Their Bolognese had chunks of beef, spicy sausage, and prosciutto. It was not your average spaghetti sauce. You can order a half-portion, and, depending on your appetizer, that would probably be plenty.

They offered some decadent desserts, including three flavors of homemade ice cream and three sorbets. They had me when they mentioned mango-orange sorbet. A large scoop came served with cookies and topped with butter-crunch toffee. It was light and packed with fresh fruit flavor. What a perfect ending!

Breakfast offerings change each morning. We started with a fresh apricot croissant. This is my idea of a perfect breakfast bread, as it only had a hint of sweetness. Our sausage-and-pepper scramble was served with home fries (soft on the inside and perfectly browned on the outside) and coffee. These innkeepers know how to spoil you.

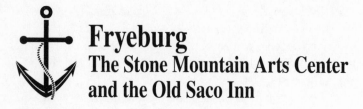

Fryeburg
The Stone Mountain Arts Center and the Old Saco Inn

The Stone Mountain Arts Center
695 Dugway Road, Brownfield
(207) 935-7292
www.stonemountainartscenter.com

The Old Saco Inn
125 Old Saco Lane, Fryeburg
(207) 925-3737
www.oldsacoinn.com

Cuisine *AMERICAN* | Minutes from *PORTLAND: 90, BANGOR: 165*

A Celtic concert and dinner at Stone Mountain Arts Center in Brownfield and a stay at the Old Saco Inn made for a great twenty-four-hour getaway. This western Maine area is beautiful, quiet, and the best place in Maine to listen to music.

Stone Mountain Arts Center

 She sings, she plays, she cooks, she inspires—Carol Noonan does it all. Eight years ago she turned an old barn into the best place to listen to music in Maine. We've been blessed to attend a couple of events each year at Stone Mountain Arts Center in Brownfield, just below Fryeburg, and they are always spectacular. Our visit in October featured an Irish band, Gaelic Storm, and they created a storm in that old barn, for sure.

We were all up and dancing, singing and cheering wildly as the band played on and on and on. The barn was jammed with folks of all ages, from youngsters to senior citizens. The lead singer was very entertaining and funny, and often got audience members into the act. The musicians were fantastic. Linda was happy we were sitting up in the balcony because she is sure I would have been onstage at some point, if not. She's probably right.

Carol has remodeled the smaller barn that serves as the first stop for guests. They expanded that barn this year, adding more tables, so it now accommodates more of the arriving guests. From five to six p.m., guests gather here, enjoy a cold beverage, and then, at six p.m., are ushered into the big barn for dinner, on a first-come, first-seated system.

The big barn seats about two hundred for dinner. On past visits, we sat on the main floor, but we arrived late this time, and the only available tables were in the balcony. At first we were disappointed, but after getting seated, we actually loved it up there. The entire place has an intimate feel, so it doesn't really matter where you sit.

The food is tasty and plentiful. I had one of my favorites, Jeff's Beef Stew, chock-full of beef chunks and vegetables with a hint of cinnamon in a hearty broth. I loved the corn bread. I ate for a half-hour and still had so much stew left that I got two more lunches out of it in the following days.

Linda raved about her lasagna. The menu is varied, ranging from pizza to salads to "SMAC 'n' Cheese" ("SMAC" stands for **Stone Mountain Arts Center**) and a corned-beef dinner. The beer and wine selection is excellent, and they serve one of my favorite Maine brews, Atlantic Brewing Company's Coal Porter.

Alison Leach—who does all sorts of jobs here, from bartending to serving—came upstairs to answer some of our food questions.

While we always enjoy our meals here, it's the music in the gorgeous old barn that draws back to Brownfield often. My only disappointment is that Stone Mountain is not closer to home.

Old Saco Inn

 I love a place where you can go to breakfast in your slippers. We slipped quietly out of our second-floor room early on Saturday morning to write in the Old Saco Inn's lovely sitting room, just off the dining room. The sitting room features wicker chairs, a gas fireplace, gorgeous chests, and old wooden floors.

I'd had to cancel a turkey hunt scheduled for that day to come here for this visit, and had felt a bit sorry for myself until we got here. Arriving about 4:30 p.m. on Friday, we were stunned as we drove in the long, winding gravel driveway to enter through lighted stone gates. I spotted kayaks and canoes stored along the river, ready for use by guests, and stopped the Subaru before we passed through the gates to jump out and take photos.

Pete and Sandi MacLachlan purchased the inn a couple of years ago, initially more than a decade ago from South Africa to travel the United States as software consultants. They "wanted to try something new while we still had the energy," according to Sandi, and focused their search for an inn to New England, with a specific list of attributes. They found them all at the Old Saco Inn.

The inn is isolated in a gorgeous and quiet setting, but very close to Fryeburg, the White Mountains, and the shopping destination of North Conway, New Hampshire. It made me think of one of my favorite T-shirts at Stone Mountain Arts Center, which reads: "SMAC in the middle of nowhere." But plenty close to somewhere!

There are three rooms in the main building that also houses their restaurant, library, and sitting room, and six suites in a separate building. We'd had trouble finding a room at the places we usually stay in this area because it was Columbus Day weekend, Carol at Stone Mountain had recommended that we try the Old Saco Inn. We were lucky to get the last available room—a small bedroom with an adjoining bathroom.

Next time we'll plan well ahead and book one of their suites, which are spacious and beautiful.

Pete has a wonderful sense of humor, and Sandi is an energetic and friendly host as well. They do it all here, from mowing the lawn to cleaning the rooms. Sandi cooks breakfasts while Pete does the serving. Sandi also cooked all the meals for the inn's dinner service for the first year, until they got so busy they hired a chef, Mark Kunick.

They serve dinner on Friday and Saturday nights year-round, with a interesting approach: one appetizer, two entrees, and one dessert, all of which change every weekend. They always have options for vegetarians and others with specific dietary needs, including gluten-free dishes, and they draw many locals who have come to appreciate this special place in their midst.

We just happened to have had the perfect fall afternoon for our drive to western Maine, passing through Sweden and Lovell. The bright blue sky put the brilliant foliage in its best light. The closer we got to New Hampshire's mountains, the more intense the colors.

But we got our biggest surprise when we drove down the Old Saco Inn driveway, passing by stately trees until we came to the opening, where we saw the impressive lodge and stone carriage house. Manicured lawns, fruit trees, and a gated entrance were set off by a white fence. It's a dramatic entrance to the peaceful property, and I'm sure most guests feel as transported as we did.

Entering the inn, incredible aromas wafted from the kitchen as they prepared for Friday night's dinner service. Both George and I regretted not having made a reservation for dinner.

The two-story open dining room was both charming and inviting. There is a screened-in porch for dining in the summertime, but in the fall they move the tables in to accommodate forty people for Friday- and Saturday-night dinners.

Chatting with owners Sandi and Pete was such a pleasure—not only to hear their story, but also to hear their wonderful South African accent. Pete took time from setting up the bar to give us a quick tour. They have painted and freshened the rooms, and have redecorated the inn with beautiful pieces of furniture and art they brought with them from South Africa.

Before breakfast on Saturday morning, we met a couple from Texas on their first visit to Maine. They were traveling New England for a foliage tour and were clearly impressed with its beauty. Shortly after, while I was getting coffee, another woman started talking to me and mentioned she was from Texas. I asked her if she'd met the other people from Texas also staying here. It turns out they were all from Houston! I introduced them, and great connections were made.

I awoke to the smell of bacon around six-thirty that morning—not a bad way to start the day! The morning's breakfast was apple pie–stuffed French toast, sausage and bacon, and fresh fruit.

The inn is just twenty short minutes from the Stone Mountain Arts Center, and even closer to North Conway—and what a gem it is!

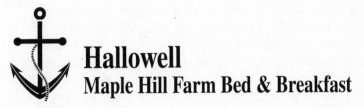

Hallowell
Maple Hill Farm Bed & Breakfast

11 Inn Road, Hallowell
(800) 622-2708; (207) 622-2708
www.maplebb.com

Minutes from *PORTLAND: 60, BANGOR: 75*

Our twenty-four-hour vacation in historic Hallowell had it all: wonderful lodging at Maple Hill Farm Bed-and-Breakfast, a superb dinner at the Liberal Cup, and a morning spent browsing in the town's many interesting shops and galleries.

I expected a great deal from Scott Cowger, a former legislator and staff member of the Department of Environmental Protection, and owner of Maple Hill Farm with his partner, Vince Hannen. Nonetheless, I was stunned by the innovative environmental systems at this remarkable B&B. The inn has received a Governor's Award for environmental excellence, was the first certified "environmental leader" green lodging establishment in Maine, and was selected as the Best Green B&B in 2011 by Yankee magazine.

I'd been wondering whether environmental investments really made a difference to travelers, and I got an answer at the Maple Hill Farm breakfast table on Saturday morning. A New York City couple, in Maine to visit their daughter at Kents Hill School, told us that they seek out green establishments when traveling, and really admire Maple Hill Farm's environmental commitment.

I also appreciated the large number of turkeys spotted in the field outside the window of our room as I enjoyed a cup of coffee Saturday morning. And here's a good example of the inn's efforts to make your stay enjoyable and unique: Scott keeps a turkey call at the front counter to entertain guests, but hadn't had any luck getting gobblers to respond. So, of course, I grabbed the call and invited him outside for a lesson. One squeak of the box call resulted in a string of loud gobbles in the nearby woods.

On our Friday-afternoon tour with Scott, it was clear that the farm's history is also an important element of this place. A piece of Hallowell granite—cut on the farm and originally used as the front steps—is now the inn's front counter.

From the inn, you can walk a woods trail to nearby Jamies Pond, protected thanks to the good work of the Kennebec Land Trust, or linger near the barn and enjoy the antics of Vince's llamas. From finding our names on the door of our room, to the sauna and hot tub just outside the inn's back door, to the fridge full of desserts, to the breakfast—everything here is designed to make your stay relaxing and special.

 I knew Maple Hill Farm was the place for me as soon as we checked in. While talking to Scott at the front counter, I noticed a small bird feeder attached to the window, offering the closest look at a chickadee or goldfinch you're likely to get!

As you drive up the steep hill to Maple Hill Farm, the first thing you'll see is a huge red barn surrounded by llamas. This is not your average B&B. The inn overlooks an enormous field bordered by beautiful stone walls. You truly feel like you have arrived at a country sanctuary.

Rooms at the inn are tastefully decorated. Every convenience is there for you—a gas fireplace, couch and nice comfy chairs, a beautiful bath with a Jacuzzi hot tub and shower, and fresh flowers on the bureau. The bathrobes provided are the most comfortable ones in the world, satin on the outside with an ultra-soft lining. Step out of the Jacuzzi and put this on and you'll know you are pampered.

We could see the 126 solar panels (and 202 tubes for hot water) on the roof from our room—it looked pretty darned cool. Along with a small wind tower, these solar panels provide 40 percent of Maple Hill's electricity.

There is a living room for guests where you'll find a library of books. The Gallery Room is used for small meetings and overflow from their two annual dinners at Easter and Mother's Day, and is filled with artwork by local artists, all of which is available for sale.

Maple Hill has another business, offering meeting spaces at their Conference Center (for 150), and Carriage House (for 50). If you've ever been to an event there, you already know that it's a beautiful spot, with fantastic food.

You will not believe the breakfast that greets you in the morning. A wood fire crackles, and muffins, juice, cereals, fruit, and coffee await. Your breakfast entree is made to order. Although pancakes, French toast, and eggs are available, we both chose to have the Eggs Benedict Arnold. The eggs come from their own chickens. I declared their eggs Benedict perfect due to amazingly crunchy English muffins and delicious hollandaise sauce.

These were twenty-four lovely hours in a great (but small) city.

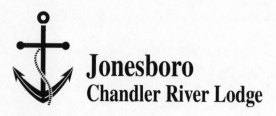

Jonesboro
Chandler River Lodge

654 US Route 1, Jonesboro
(207) 434-2540
www.chandlerriverlodge.com

Cuisine *AMERICAN* | Minutes from *PORTLAND: 210, BANGOR: 100*

Discovering the Chandler River Lodge is like finding a huge piece of sea glass. You just want to bring it home with you! Tucked up on a knoll well off Route 1 in Jonesboro sits a beautiful historic home (circa 1797) that is now a B&B and restaurant, with uncrowded awesome beaches close by.

 One of the great things about traveling around our state is finding places that are so special—some of which we'd never heard of. Such is the case with the Chandler River Lodge, which we've been driving by for years on our way to Lubec.

Emily Fitzsimmons has to be one of the most energetic, organized, and busy people I have met. She is the chef at this fine dining establishment, but it turns out that is not her only responsibility. She also takes reservations, greets guests, creates menus, cooks dinners, prepares and serves breakfast, and even cleans the rooms! Not to mention she has four young children. But you would never guess she has so much on her plate by her easygoing, can-do attitude.

We stayed in the Hannah Weston Room, a light, tastefully decorated space that included a TV, coffeepot, and desk with a wrought-iron base. Wallpapered walls were decorated with artwork, and above the bed hung a collection of gorgeous old clocks. Layers of linens were on the bed: luxurious sheets, cotton blanket, comforter, and an intricate bedspread. And atop all of this rested a folded quilt.

Our suite had a large bathroom. Terrycloth robes were hanging nearby, making us feel pampered by the variety of bath products and number of towels. Lace curtains over the glass-paned door gave it that older-home coziness.

The dining room (which is open for dinner on Friday and Saturday nights) continues the colonial feel of this house through its wallpaper, lace curtains, refinished wooden floors, and fireplace. White-cloth-covered tables are set with an extensive amount of silverware and candles. It is a fine place for friends to gather or for a romantic evening out.

Emily is free to create whatever she wants here, and changes the menu every four weeks or so. Linda Patryn, our server, shares the history of the house with ease. It turns out that she worked on the history of Jonesboro, so she is very knowledgeable. Both Emily and Linda are Jonesboro natives.

We ordered an appetizer and an entree, but the surprise here was the hidden courses that come out as well. The small amuse-bouche (whatever bite-size taste the chef wants to create to please your mouth) that evening was a tiny crepe filled with blueberry, Gouda, and pulled pork. One bite and we knew it was going to be a special meal.

We ordered the bacon-and-blue-cheese-stuffed mushrooms, and out came a beautiful long narrow dish with seven stuffed mushrooms. This was a great choice for sharing, just as the two ladies at the next table were doing. Our two favorite ingredients came in a creamy stuffing of baby portabellas. Enough said.

We also ordered the bruschetta topped with fresh basil pesto, Parmesan, and tomatoes, and finished with aged balsamic vinegar to lend some sweetness. Delightful. Next out was a salad and tasty house-made sweet focaccia bread.

When I found out that Emily makes the pasta, my decision for a main course was made—the Lodge Pasta. The fresh, wide fettuccine pasta comes with a garlic cream sauce, which is delicious, and can be topped with shrimp, beef, or, my choice—grilled chicken. It was a lovely pasta dish, and I continued to enjoy it reheated as leftovers after we returned home.

We can tell we are full when George does not persist in his quest for dessert. He'd earlier asked our server what would happen if he wanted dessert now that his four forks were already used. She assured him she would bring him whatever he needed. Turns out he needed nothing. We were too full for another bite—at least until breakfast the next morning.

Linda hasn't got that dessert anecdote quite right. I didn't order anything, but two friendly ladies at the next table—after I asked them if I could photograph their dessert—shared it with me!

Poking through the Lodge's guestbook, I noted that folks from all over this country and Canada have stayed and/or eaten here, and from all over Maine—but it was the number of visitors from local towns that explained how the restaurant can remain open year-round. I noted guests from Machias, Milbridge, Jonesport, Beals, Cutler, East Machias, and Steuben. We'd recently been in Lubec, and a lady there told me she and her friends drive all the way to Jonesboro just to eat dinner here.

While they do accept drop-in guests, reservations are strongly suggested for both rooms and dinner. When they don't have reservations, they sometimes choose not to be open that day or night. They also do a lot of catering, hosting weddings and special celebrations inside and outside the inn.

I loved this place so much that I took eleven pages of notes. There's no way to convey all of this to you, but here's a short version.

I loved Emily, her amazing work ethic, her smile and stories, and her enthusiasm for her family. "My husband is awesome!" she exclaimed when I asked how she could do so much. The entire family was scheduled to begin raking blueberries in their own fields the following week.

I loved Emily's cooking. She graduated from Eastern Maine Technical College's culinary school, cooked at another nearby inn, a couple of restaurants, and Washington Academy for eight years before taking on the Chandler River Lodge three and a half years ago. She lives right across the road.

I loved our server. Linda Patryn's historical knowledge and stories were outstanding. Not only that, but she handled the entire room, and, when someone stepped in from outside to inquire about a room, she also took them upstairs to show them the only vacant room. Linda does it all, just like Emily. They are a great team!

I loved the setting. It is far back off Route 1, with a small pond and lots of lawn overlooking the Chandler River.

I loved the history. Hannah Weston's story was framed on the wall in our room. Hannah helped drive the British away when they attacked Machias in 1775.

I loved our dinner. And I wasn't the only one.

"This is wonderful!" I heard a lady exclaim at a nearby table. Later, at another table, a guest in a party of four turned to her friend and said, "Thank you, Steve. Great choice of restaurants!"

Beginning with a Cellardoor Winery (our favorite in Lincolnville) Cantina Rossa, a nice red blend, to enjoying the tasty *amuse-bouche*, slowing down on the salad and bread—getting too full! and then having my palate cooled by a nice drop of blueberry sorbet—I staggered on to the entree—the Sam Watts. Emily likes to use the names of local historical figures for some of her dishes. The Sam Watts was a seafood-stuffed haddock with crab, shrimp, and scallops, served with a tomato beurre blanc. I've enjoyed haddock dishes all over Maine, and I can tell you, this one is exceptional. I was in sea-food heaven. I even enjoyed the carrot puree that came with it. I told Emily it was good enough to bring Sam Watts back from the dead.

Later, when I told Linda I was glad we didn't have dessert, she responded, "Oh my gosh, I wish I had a tape recorder."

We took our remaining wine to the deck to enjoy the cool evening and sparkling, nearly full moon shining on the river. Serene. We are dreaming of a return to this special place and these special people.

Just south of Jonesboro you will find two of our favorite places: Roque Bluffs State Park and Jasper Beach. At Roque Bluffs, there's an inland water pond for swimming with a picnic area, and across the road lies one of the state's most beautiful (and always uncrowded) fine sand beaches.

After a brief walk around the park, we drove on to Jasper Beach in Bucks Harbor. We hadn't been there in years, but remembered the astonishingly smooth stones and stunning views. We got confused by the route, saw a lot of the peninsula, and finally found Jasper Beach, where we enjoyed a wonderful picnic, sharing the huge beach with just ten other people.

Kingfield
One Stanley Avenue Restaurant and Three Stanley Avenue Bed & Breakfast

Stanley Avenue, Kingfield
(207) 265-5541
www.stanleyavenue.com

Cuisine *AMERICAN / EUROPEAN* | Minutes from *PORTLAND: 125, BANGOR: 160*

The two Stanley Avenue attractions offer a step back in time. Owner and chef Dan Davis opened the inn and restaurant in 1972, and is very busy during the winter, serving skiers from nearby Sugarloaf Mountain. The restaurant is located at One Stanley Avenue, while next door, at Three Stanley Avenue, you'll find six charming rooms in a large Victorian house.

Chef and owner Dan Davis, who lives with his wife Susan upstairs at One Stanley, has poured his life into this historic building that includes his impressive collection of stained glass in the windows and walls.

For dinner, our server Tammy seated us in "the Arch," the first of two intimate dining rooms. Tammy owns a preschool center in Phillips, so she and I had a lot to talk about. The tin ceilings in this room are intricate. Bathed in rose pink, the rooms are romantically lit with candles on the tables, and there is quiet music in the background. One look around and you know you are in for an extraordinary meal here.

One whiff of their warm fresh wheat bread will have you swooning. Chef Davis grinds his own wheat. His European travels have influenced the type of food he serves here, but he melds this with the flavors of Maine. So fiddleheads meet juniper berries and hemlock, and meats such as duck, rabbit, lobster, and venison are classically prepared. But classic does not mean boring. The dishes are beautiful, and the flavors pop.

Entrees come with bread, a mixed-greens salad served with house-made dressing, fresh vegetables, rice, potato, or Shaker dumplings, and coffee or tea. This is an opportunity for gourmet food at reasonable prices.

I started my meal with artichoke hearts. It was a simple dish of three artichoke hearts with an amazingly light, fresh basil dressing—a perfect appetizer, and one I have never seen on a menu elsewhere. It's one of those dishes I will end up craving.

My entree, the Beef and Chestnut Pie, was another unusual dish, served in an oval dish encased in gorgeous pastry. Chunks of beef tenderloin combine with chestnuts and mushrooms and rest in a heavenly gravy. Two of the ingredients listed were molasses and garlic, so maybe that is the secret of the sauce. I was only able to eat half, but it was almost as pretty coming out of my own kitchen as leftovers. When they wrapped it up for me to take home, they formed a swan out of the aluminum foil. No detail is overlooked.

Three Stanley Avenue, next door to the restaurant, is Dan Davis's six-room Victorian B&B. I would describe the decor as tasteful simplicity. Patterned lace sheers hang on the windows between shades and curtains, and the effect of white on white is stunning. A wicker love seat with patterned cushions and pillows sits beside an antique free-standing clothes rack. The bed is covered with pretty quilts and pillows that are softer than soft. There is no TV here.

At breakfast the next morning the sun streamed through five panels of stained glass. We were seated on the porch. Dan had the border of narrow transom windows specially made. We were treated to fresh coffee poured out of a silver pot, orange juice, and blueberry pancakes with syrup.

Just when I thought my day couldn't get off to a better start, Dan asked if we would like to see his remodeled kitchen. Dan's ingenious ideas are showcased here. Three skylights flood the space with light, and a metal rack is filled with pans and utensils. He has incorporated a cooler from an old general store in Canaan. Half of the cooler opens in his kitchen while the other side opens into the walk-in cooler. An antique cabinet has been repurposed into the end of the island. The two gigantic ovens are the original ones he's been using since 1972.

Stanley Avenue can accommodate special occasions such as rehearsal dinners and parties for up to thirty. They even have a restored gazebo and spacious lawns for outdoor weddings. But if you are looking for an special meal, hurry to Kingfield.

I love many things about One Stanley Avenue, opened by Dan Davis in 1972. It's a step back to the days of unhurried dining. The food is exceptional and chef Dan is personable and interesting. We chose to stay in Dan's inn next door. And I'm glad we did because it gave us a chance to step away from the TV, computer, chores, and other things that keep us busy at home. Yes, the inn offers Wi-Fi, but we chose not to go online that night. The rooms are a bargain, and close enough to Sugarloaf to attract skiers. The snowmobile trail runs behind the inn's four wooded acres, making this a wonderful overnight stop for traveling snowmobilers.

Arriving at the restaurant at 6:30 p.m., we were invited by Dan to enjoy a drink in the lounge. It's a lovely living room featuring a piano and antique furniture, with family photos spread throughout, and a bar tucked in the far corner. On this evening, the steady tick of a grandfather clock was the only sound in the room. What a great place to relax! Tammy, who served us throughout the evening, recommended a St. Francis Cabernet Sauvignon, which was really good.

Dan came out of the kitchen briefly to visit with us, and we were delighted to discover we had many friends in common.

It's really no surprise that Dan is an accomplished and creative chef. He traveled the world in his earlier life, cooking all over Europe and the United States, sometimes with famous chefs. But he has made the menu at One Stanley Avenue his own, calling it classic cuisine of Maine. He even forages for some of his ingredients.

I began with delicious smoked Maine mussels featuring Dan's grandmother's dill dressing. Best mussels I've ever tasted. I passed the dish to Lin, who took a big bite and exclaimed, "Oh my God, that's lemony!" She'd grabbed a chunk of the lemon along with the mussel.

I was tempted by the beef dishes, but Linda insisted I be more adventurous, so I ordered the Saged Rabbit with Raspberry Sauce, added to the menu in 1986. The rabbit comes from a local farm, and is served in thin slices wrapped in duck skin. I've eaten a lot of rabbit over the years, but nothing this imaginative and tasty. And as Tammy told us, "We don't provide sharp knives. Everything can be cut with a butter knife." The dumpling must be experienced. I loved the texture.

I insisted on dessert, "so we can get a photo," and Linda ordered the Raspberry Crème—their smallest dessert, but a perfect ending to our meal.

We adjourned again to the lounge—I just love that space—to visit with Dan and his wife.

The next morning, after a wonderful breakfast, Dan told us he will keep the inn and restaurant going for a few more years until he turns eighty.

"It's home," he said. "If it doesn't work, I've still got my home."

Lincolnville
The Youngtown Inn & Restaurant

581 Youngtown Road, Lincolnville
Inn: (207) 763-4290
Restaurant: (800) 291-8438
www.youngtowninn.com

Cuisine *FRENCH* | Minutes from *PORTLAND: 105, BANGOR: 70*

A touch of French elegance in an historic Maine building makes The Youngtown Inn and Restaurant exceptional and popular. The French restaurant is a treat in Maine, and Camden State Park is across the road.

The Lincolnville Book Festival, where I was invited to speak about my book, *A Life Lived Outdoors*, gave us our first opportunity to write about the town, and the minute we saw a photo of The Youngtown Inn, we knew that it was the place for us.

We love historic inns, but this one surprised us. In the Young family for about 180 years, it was purchased by a non-family member and converted to an inn in the early 1980s. Manuel and MaryAnn Mercier purchased it in 1991, turning it into the place where they raised their three boys, a welcoming inn, and an amazing restaurant.

MaryAnn is friendly, and we shared stories throughout our stay. I loved her story about the boys, who objected to the move to Maine from New Jersey, but when they got older, thanked her. We'll be thanking her for a long time for giving us such a wonderful experience—a combination of the best of Maine and the best of France.

You'll see this combination everywhere, from the dining-room curtains, purchased on one of many of Manuel and Mary-Ann's visits to France, to the wide pine boards throughout the inn. Enjoying an early-morning cup of coffee in the second-floor sitting room, I spotted two books: *Memories of Camden,* and *Provence—The Beautiful Cookbook.*

After my Friday-afternoon book talk at **Beyond the Sea**, Nanette Gionfriddo's shop full of books and art, clothes and dishes and more, we crossed the street to enjoy the ocean view from Lincolnville's busy beach. I noticed a new pub, opened by the folks at **Andrew's Brewery**—a particular favorite of mine. Alas, we had no opportunity to eat there.

So we drove the five miles to the inn, tucked just outside Camden State Park. A gorgeous male cardinal welcomed us in the parking lot.

We had no idea the state park stretched this far from its entrance on Route 1 in Camden, nor did we know there are so many great trails into the park from this side of it. MaryAnn suggested a pre-dinner hike to Maiden Cliff that started right at the inn and ended on top of a hill with an astonishing view and a huge crop of wild blueberries. They were so sweet, but I was glad we didn't bring a bucket, because Linda would have stayed there picking for hours.

At breakfast the next morning, MaryAnn escorted us to a table already set with fruit, sticky buns, and fresh flowers. Manuel prepared a wonderful dish—scrambled eggs on a toasted muffin and topped with smoked salmon. Yum! We lingered and laughed while visiting with a young couple at the next table.

While the breakfast was terrific, it's Friday night's dinner that I will never forget. With guidance from our server, Michael, who has worked here since the Merciers purchased the inn (while also pursuing two college degrees), I chose Pâté de Foie de Canard for an appetizer (duck mousse and port pâté with cornichons and toast points). Michael explained the dish to me after I told him I was entirely incapable of describing it. The texture and taste of the smooth pâté was superb, and the sharp, sour pickles added extra flavor. Michael said it was aspic along the side of the pâté—something I'd never seen before.

Stymied by the entree selections, I was leaning toward a duck-breast dish with green peppercorn, brandy, and cream (making it a "ducky" night), but Michael talked me into Chef Manuel's "signature dish," Carré d'Agneau aux Herbes de Provence (roast rack of lamb).

It was not only a work of art, but the tender lamb, flavored with rosemary, and a from-scratch sauce, was a dining delight. I also enjoyed the potato cake, crispy green beans in a buttery sauce, and carrots.

"What do you taste in the carrots?" asked Linda.

"Vanilla," I answered.

"Holy cow, I think you got it," she exclaimed.

Well, almost. Michael said it was maple.

The charming Youngtown Inn is just up the road from **Cellardoor Winery** in Lincolnville. It's only a few miles from downtown Camden, but has a much different ambience—calm and peaceful, with a strong sense of history. Our room was light and cheerful with a hint of European style.

We felt immediately welcomed after a short visit with MaryAnn. You can see just how much she and Manuel love their home and the business they have built together. They appreciate the specialness of Maine people and the area they now call home.

One of the great reasons to visit here is the inn's award-winning restaurant. Manuel is a French chef and has stayed true to his roots by offering stunning French dishes that are not intimidating. MaryAnn calls him a "classically trained saucier."

"It's all about the sauces in French cooking," she says, adding that Manuel makes each sauce individually when the dish is ordered.

I started my meal with gazpacho, and impressive it was, served in a distinctive square bowl and topped with fresh crabmeat, which certainly elevated this simple soup. It had a kick from chilies, but I could still taste the cucumber, green pepper, and tomatoes—perfection when paired with the crunchy French rolls and small bottle of olive oil on the table.

Though the interior dining room is gorgeous, we sat on the porch this night. White tablecloths, fresh flowers, and pale walls accented with white woodwork create a relaxing space.

My entree of filet of beef was embellished with caramelized onions and Roquefort. The rich demi-glace served with my filet makes one have the uncivilized urge to lick the plate. It took all my willpower to resist that urge.

I'd read that the crème brûlée was a signature dessert here, so I didn't even really listen to the list recited by Michael. It was served at room temperature. And its texture was creamy, not as solid as others I'd eaten before. Its crunchy sugar topping and distinctive vanilla flavor made it a memorable dessert.

The common room of this beautiful inn is on the second floor. Wainscoting and beautiful molding accent the beige-on-white color scheme. You'll find a desk to work at, two chairs, and a couch for leisurely visiting. French artwork decorates the walls, and you can choose your form of entertainment, from DVDs and games to books and brochures about the area. It's an inviting space, and I'm certain that I am not the first guest to spot the cookies sitting next to the coffeemaker.

Breakfast is served from eight to nine a.m., so I came early to have a cup of coffee. It was a style of coffeemaker I'd never seen before, so I'm sure I must have looked pretty funny trying to figure out how the coffee pouches with a round plastic top fit into that machine. Luckily the instructions were in both French and English and had little pictures to guide me. I was rewarded with a great cup of coffee.

Breakfast here is special, as well. It's the picture of a country inn when you enter to find tables tastefully set, awaiting overnight guests. Start with coffee, juice, and fresh fruit—that morning, a presentation of cantaloupe revealed the innkeepers' exquisite attention to detail.

The warm entree was creamy scrambled eggs served atop a potato cake, with roasted peppers on the side. The bready texture and chives made a lovely savory dish. I opted not to have the smoked salmon that topped George's dish.

Warm hospitality and fantastic food in a comfortable, relaxing setting—The Youngtown Inn is a very special place indeed.

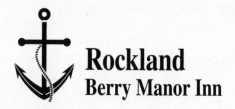

Rockland
Berry Manor Inn

81 Talbot Avenue, Rockland
(800) 774-5692, (207) 596-7696
www.berrymanorinn.com

Minutes from *PORTLAND: 100, BANGOR: 105*

Berry Manor Inn is artistic, historic, and very welcoming, in a town on the ocean with a major art gallery, lots of shops, restaurants, and access to awesome spots all along and off the coast.

It has been a couple of years since we stayed at the Berry Manor Inn in Rockland, but it always feels like going home. The staff here is warm and welcoming.

We visited while the beautiful Christmas decorations were up, which is indeed a sight to see. Stair railings and doorways are decked out in greenery, ribbons, antique items, pinecones, and berries. A stunningly perfect Christmas tree with a Victorian theme sits in the parlor.

Owners Mike LaPosta and Cheryl Michaelsen, who have a playful sense of humor, do everything with a wink and a nod. On the second floor an upside-down Christmas tree hangs from the light in the middle of the sitting room. On the third floor we found a sparse tree loaded with maroon pears and gold tassels and a white partridge sitting at the top.

Antique chairs and couches are sprinkled throughout the inn. I've found that most old chairs are hard and stiff, pretty to look at but not to sit in. They've chosen seating that you sink into, close your eyes, and smile. It begs you to rest and relax. Guests seem to occupy the living spaces more than we see at other inns. Maybe it's the subliminal message one gets due to the hospitality here. You feel like making yourself at home.

The inn always has a variety of pies (berry, of course) available for guests. Out on the counter in the inn's kitchen or in the gathering room of the Carriage House, you will find two or three varieties of fruit pies. The pies are not pre-cut, so you can let your conscience be your guide as to how big a slice you take. Unfortunately for George, I was the one wielding the knife. I appeased his complaints by reminding him that there was ice cream in the freezer to go with his pie.

This visit we stayed in the Children's Room on the third floor. There are eight rooms in the main inn, and four in the Carriage House, all furnished Victorian-style. Each room has a sign signifying how the room was used when the Berry family owned it in the 1800s. This home has been an inn for over a century, and there are not too many places that can say that.

The breakfasts here are something to look forward to. The next day's menu is on a table in the hallway when you enter. When I woke up the first morning I could smell the cinnamon and sugar of that day's offerings. A choice of juices, coffee, and a fruit cup were brought right out by our server, Jordan.

We had dug into our fruit and George had already eaten part of his muffin before I realized we had not taken a picture—something we try to do at each place we visit.

"You forgot the presentation," Cheryl said when she noticed we were trying to re-create our fruit dish. Smiling, she pointed out the fresh mint leaves we'd removed. We retook the picture but missed the placement of blueberries in the middle of the mint. Remember that attention to detail I mentioned earlier?

My raspberry muffin was quite possibly the best muffin I have ever eaten. Its crunchy top gave way to a soft interior filled with luscious raspberries. I could not eat it all, but guarded it carefully to finish later.

Cheryl's brown-sugar-topped cinnamon French toast must have been what I smelled when I woke up. It resembled a bread pudding in texture, and from the ohhh's and ahhh's around the room, clearly everyone in the dining room enjoyed it as much as we did.

 For the past sixteen years, Cheryl Michaelsen and Mike LaPosta have offered a high level of comfort, hospitality with a sense of humor, and a real interest in making sure guests enjoy all that this region of the coast can provide—all while staying at their beautiful, historic Victorian inn in a quiet Rockland neighborhood. And I haven't yet mentioned the pies! Blueberry, raspberry, and cherry pies were available—at all times—in the downstairs dining room during our late-December visit. And yes, we indulged, both nights, although as Linda reported, she cut the slices, which were very modest.

I hope to do better when we stop at the inn during the eleventh annual Pies on Parade fund-raiser, held in January, to support the local food bank and fuel assistance program. About three dozen inns, restaurants, and businesses offer sweet and savory pies that afternoon. We'll be sure to start our adventure at Berry Manor Inn for a piece of berry pie before we get filled up.

The inn includes several common rooms, both large and small, where you can relax and linger, as well as a dining room. All of the inn's guest rooms are special. Most are in the inn, but we also like the rooms in the adjacent Carriage House. They all share a sense of style, from the imaginative art to the seating. We enjoyed our room's gas fireplace both nights.

But it was when we went upstairs after enjoying our pie on the first night that I was really impressed. In our room, someone had switched on a few lights, turned down the bed, closed the curtains, started some music, replaced the towels, and left us chocolates.

Breakfasts are special occasions, with wonderful food and lots of humor. We were blessed by the appearance of Cheryl's mom, Ally Taylor. She's a real entertainer, and presented a skit entitled Bird Calls that was hilarious and a bit ribald. Around the room, guests visited with each other. It's just that kind of place.

We'd had a delightful conversation with two couples the night before, in the living room, after we had returned from dinner at our favorite Rockland restaurant, **Cafe Miranda**. The ladies were working on a puzzle and Linda joined right in.

On our first morning, I dropped downstairs to ask Cheryl a question and noticed that assistant innkeeper Alyssa, a college student, was offering guests a few tips on what to do in the area. We heard about so many places to visit that I told her we might need to stay the entire week to get to them all.

Here are the two favorites we visited that day: We were wowed by the Shaker exhibit at the **Farnsworth Art Museum**, and also enjoyed the paintings of Andrew Wyeth. The Farnsworth is a must-see whenever you are in Rockland.

We were also very impressed by the new Maine Coastal Islands National Wildlife Refuge Visitor Center, a project of the US Fish and Wildlife Service.

Back at the Inn after dinner at **3Crow** on our second night, we had a nice visit with Cheryl, who told us how important elopement weddings are to their business. There was a wedding scheduled the next afternoon.

At breakfast the next morning, I noticed this on my Berry Manor Inn coffee cup: "Experience a return to graciousness and grandeur." The Inn is certainly that, and more.

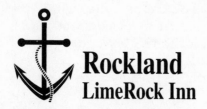

Rockland
LimeRock Inn

96 Limerock Street, Rockland
(800) 546-3762, (207) 594-2257
www.LimeRockInn.com

Minutes from *PORTLAND: 100, BANGOR: 95*

The LimeRock Inn has been twice choosen by Down East magazine readers as Best B&B. The Inn is historic, the grounds are quiet, and you are only a five-minute walk to downtown Rockland, with its wonderful art galleries, shops, and restaurants, and, of course, the ocean.

Frank came out of the kitchen where he was preparing our breakfast to introduce two unacquainted couples from London, England, to each other. Before long, the couples were seated together, engaged in eager conversation—not unlike the conversation Linda and I were enjoying with a couple from Rhode Island, who we met hanging out in the kitchen the day before. They are regular guests here after becoming fast friends with the LimeRock's owners, Frank and PJ, on their very first trip five years ago.

This may be the friendliest B&B in the state. This was our second visit, and Frank and PJ greeted us on the wonderful wrap-around porch (*Yankee Magazine* Editor's Choice for Best Wrap-around Porch in 2011), where we spent twenty minutes catching up on each other's news. This inn is elegant and historic, comfortable and quiet, but it's the innkeepers that make it so special.

You would never guess you are just two blocks from the hustle and bustle of one of our favorite downtowns. We walked to Rockland's Main Street, full of superb art galleries (including the Farnsworth Museum), shops, and restaurants. Then we drove the short distance to Owls Head Lighthouse to enjoy the stunning ocean scenery.

We had planned to have lunch at our favorite restaurant, **Cafe Miranda**, but Frank's breakfast was so filling, we weren't hungry. The last time we stayed here, we left before sunrise to catch a ferry to Monhegan and missed breakfast. Boy, what a mistake that was. We made up for it this trip by enjoying two spectacular breakfasts at the inn.

We slept late on our first morning, and Linda slipped out to the pantry to make coffee in the Keurig machine. But Frank was already busy at work in the kitchen and gave Linda two hot cups of coffee, telling her, "It's better than Keurig."

Our Island Cottage room, on the first floor at the back of the inn, included a private deck with stairs to the beautiful grounds out back. We enjoyed our coffee on the deck, admiring PJ's gorgeous flower gardens, watching cardinals, cedar wax-wings, and goldfinches, when Linda said, "Now this is a civilized morning—no newspapers."

"Well, I was just going to ask Frank or PJ if they have today's newspaper," I responded. We didn't get a paper, but not to worry—the inn has Wi-Fi so I was able to read my *Kennebec Journal* online.

The backyard is nicely screened by trees, and the Inn's next-door neighbors match Frank and PJ in well-kept lawns, providing a restful setting for our peaceful morning.

We had previously stayed at the LimeRock Inn in 2011, and had been itching to return ever since. This time, Frank and PJ met us on the porch, where we talked so long that we made Frank late for his city council meeting. When they led us to the Island Cottage room on the first floor, I instantly recognized it as the one we saw, and fell in love with, when we stopped in here for the Pies on Parade fundraiser one winter.

With its blue and light yellow color scheme and white woodwork, one feels the cheeriness of the room immediately. Wicker chairs, a bead-board bed frame, a section of shingled wall, and double French doors leading to the deck and backyard make you feel like you are indeed in a cottage. The bath included a whirlpool tub.

The very comfortable king-size bed with Egyptian cotton bedding and hypoallergenic pillows had us sleeping until 7:30 a.m.—unheard of for us! The coffee was already brewed and waiting for us in the pantry as Frank busily worked on a spectacular breakfast.

Our small porch beckoned. Enjoying coffee here in the comfy cushioned chairs overlooking the peaceful backyard starts one's day off right. The flower garden was in full bloom, and large trees surrounding the yard provided an oasis that birds took advantage of.

PJ set us up with a carafe of orange juice and brought coffee in beautiful mugs with a picture of the inn painted on them. Their special Rock City coffee blend is superb. Fresh fruit served in martini glasses comes next: strawberries, blueberries, and whipped cream one morning, melon and blueberries the next.

Frank gets up early to bake delectable creations. The light airy biscuits had guests swooning, as did the tiny banana-pecan mini muffins. Most B&Bs would stop there, but this inn provides a full breakfast. They vary the entrees by alternating sweet and savory. Frank's lemon-blueberry pancakes the first morning were delicious—not overly sweet—as was the frittata with sausage I had the second morning.

Frank said he tries to offer "affordable luxury and comfortable elegance." The fact that both tourists and Mainers alike stay here, often at the recommendation of friends, and that 50 percent of their guests are repeat customers, tells you the things they are doing at the LimeRock Inn are working.

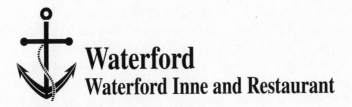

Waterford
Waterford Inne and Restaurant

258 Chadbourne Road, Waterford
(207) 542-3630, (207) 583-4037
www.waterfordinne.com

Cuisine *AMERICAN* | Minutes from *PORTLAND: 80, BANGOR: 150*

There are no distractions here like Wi-Fi. There is a TV in the library, but watching it, as Linda noted, "would be wrong." They are busiest in the summer and fall. And they don't take credit cards, so bring cash or a check.

I love traveling to western Maine during any season, but the rolling hills covered in snow make a particularly impressive sight. I wasn't sure where the town of Waterford was, but it turns out to be only about fifteen minutes west of Norway.

We turned onto Chadbourne Road and drove up the steep hill until we reached the Waterford Inne's beautiful property. This 1800s farmhouse has been lovingly turned into a Registry Select Inn by Barbara Vanderzanden.

Barbara and her mother, now deceased, started this inn back in 1978. She and her mom were avid travelers, eventually visiting all of the continents. The inn is now chockablock full of memorabilia from around the world. The scale of attention to detail in decorating is hard to imagine. In every corner of every room, you are drawn in by beautiful things. Art comes in a variety of forms here—from books and carvings to prints and paintings. Clearly Barbara has exquisite taste and a keen eye. You will find yourself constantly discovering something you overlooked before.

We were met at the door by Barbara . . . on crutches. She had traveled to ski in France about a month earlier, and broke her leg on the very first day! But we were soon to find out through visiting with her and her partner, Jan Beckwermert, that very little can slow this woman down. We had wonderful conversations before and after dinner, and again at breakfast the next morning. They are clearly suited for the hospitality business. By the end of breakfast, with laughter and conversation still easily flowing, I felt as if I'd known them my whole life!

There are eight rooms at the inn, each with its own theme and personality. My words alone are not going to give this inn the justice it deserves. It sits on twenty-five acres of wooded property, and Jan told me she mows four acres of lawns!

We were the only guests at the inn on a Monday in late February, so to say we were feeling a bit pampered as we stepped into the great room to see our candlelit table readied for dinner, with a fire crackling in the fireplace, would be an understatement. Jan served us our four-course dinner while Barbara helped cook in the kitchen. (Yes, of course she had figured out how to stand at the stove and work on crutches.) Weathered barn boards and exposed beams combine with subtle blue woodwork and pops of color in the many artifacts on display.

Warm rolls and a bowl of incredible watercress and walnut soup began our meal. It was one of the best soups I have eaten in a very long time—a definite keeper, and the perfect antidote to a blustery evening outside. The next course was a salad of fruits on a bed of baby spinach. The flavors of kiwi, watermelon, strawberry, and banana were delicious when topped with poppy-seed dressing.

The main course that night was rack of lamb. The mild and tender lamb became extraordinary with a crusty rosemary rub. Golden roasted potatoes, a baked version of baby zucchini with tarragon, and steamed cauliflower rounded out the meal. The food is very good, and you will not go away hungry when you dine here.

We settled in front of the fire to enjoy conversation and dessert, a raspberry crumble with a shortbread topping. What a very fine meal.

Reservations are required, and the restaurant is open to the public, too, not just reserved for guests. But when you stay at the inn, it's only about ten steps from dinner to your room!

 I had to jam on the brakes to avoid a flock of turkeys crossing the inn's driveway when we arrived, so of course, I later asked Barbara if turkey was on the dinner menu that night. Jan offered me a gun if I wanted to shoot my own dinner, but I demurred. Maybe on our next visit.

Entering the Chesapeake Room, focused on waterfowl paintings and carvings, I felt right at home, immediately spying a State of Maine duck print by one of my favorite painters, Jeannine Staples. The room has a bed, a wooden chest, two chairs where I spent some time reading, a chest of drawers, a large and well-lit bathroom, and a Franklin stove, all ready to light. Even the tray holding wine and other glasses had a painting of a duck on it.

I took about a hundred photos while wandering through the inn. The art and collectibles are stunning. I was particularly captivated by Ted Hanks's tiny carved geese on the fireplace mantle in the living room.

Our dinner was one I shall never forget. It featured special touches like cloth napkins, colorful cloth coasters, and even a beautiful bread basket. While the soup was tasty—hearty without being filling, and perfect on this wintry evening—my attention wandered as I surveyed the room. Overhead, carved birds and woven baskets hung from the old rafters.

The fruit salad included all of my favorites: watermelon, banana, strawberries, kiwi, and a variety of greens with a sweet dressing. Yum.

The lamb, with potatoes and zucchini, was beautifully arranged and delicious. Surprisingly, I loved the zucchini. Jan said they baked it for twenty-five minutes, then dipped it in butter. It had a licorice taste, which caused Linda to note, as I was raving about it, "You always say you don't like licorice!"

The ice cream dessert provided a very nice finish as we gathered around the fire. Throughout our visit, the opportunity to talk with Barbara and Jan really made our stay something special. Barbara regaled us with stories about her worldwide trips with her mother, and both ladies shared stories about their recent travel adventures. We skipped around the world, stopping for a while in Barbara's favorite place, South Africa (she is fascinated by nature and animals—giving the two of us a lot to talk about!). Her last adventure with her mother was to Antarctica.

The inn is just fifteen minutes from another one of our very favorite restaurants, **76 Pleasant** in Norway, thirty minutes from our favorite place to listen to music, **Stone Mountain Arts Center** in Brownfield, and close to North Conway's shopping mecca. It's in the midst of a major recreational area of lakes, mountains, skiing, great fishing, and a lot more. I wish we'd had time to try the snowshoe trail that begins right at the inn, but a snowstorm Tuesday morning sent us scurrying home.

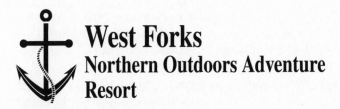

West Forks
Northern Outdoors Adventure Resort

1771 Route 201, The Forks
(800) 765-7238, (207) 663-4466
www.northernoutdoors.com

Cuisine *AMERICAN* | Minutes from *PORTLAND: 140, BANGOR: 105*

The Kennebec River that flows through Skowhegan, Waterville, Augusta, and Gardiner starts its journey just north of West Forks. The journey to West Forks on a scenic highway delivers you to Northern Outdoors, Maine's first rafting company, and now a sprawling resort of log buildings with all the amenities and luxuries you seek in a vacation. In a two-day, one-night adventure, we spent half a day fishing, a whole day rafting, enjoyed meals and a very nice cabin, toured their brewery, got to know some great people, and learned a lot about this interesting region of Maine.

I first rafted the Kennebec River gorge over thirty years ago, and Suzie Hockmeyer was my guide. It was a trip I've never forgotten, and I've been trying to get Linda to try it ever since. Today Northern Outdoors, co-owned by Russell Walters and Suzie, is still known for its rafting trips, but the business has diversified into a year-round resort offering numerous outdoor experiences, including snowmobiling, ATV riding, fishing, and hunting.

They've got accommodations for every taste, with 250 beds nestled in gorgeous cabins, and another 150 in outdoor venues right on the river. The pool, hot tub, and game room are always in use.

Downstairs in Northern's lodge is the **Kennebec River Brewery**, where owner Jim Yearwood and manager Mike McConnell craft exceptional beer each year, most of it consumed on the premises. I've never forgotten the tasty porter I enjoyed the first year the brewery opened, and I was pleased to discover they've actually improved it by adding a smoky taste. It's got a fairly high alcohol level, so it's best to walk from your cabin to the lodge to imbibe!

I've fished with him before, and can report from experience that Chris Russell of Caratunk is one of Maine's top guides. Although he takes his clients "anyplace there are fish to catch," the name of his business, Kennebec River Angler, makes it clear where his favorite water is.

Our half-day float-and-fish trip on the Kennebec started in West Forks, a scenic stretch that reminds me of some of my favorite Montana rivers. We had a great time, caught three species of fish, and introduced Linda to drift-boat fishing. She loved it.

She also loved Chris's three-weight Sage Flight rod and Ross Evolution Reel with sharkskin line. That may cost me a lot of money.

Summertime in Maine—is there really any better place to be? I want to be outside enjoying every minute of it. Gardening, taking walks, and even mowing the lawn makes me happy because I'm outside. Now these sound like chores to George, so he tries to take me away to do "fun" things.

People often ask if I fish; everyone knows how obsessive George can be about fishing. So the answer is "yes," I do fish. But truthfully, it involves a lot of help. So a half-day guided fishing trip down the Kennebec sounded good to me. I couldn't quite picture a drift boat. When he explained it was rubber, I was a little concerned. I shouldn't have worried.

Picture a perfect summer day, an expert guide paddling us downriver in a comfy raft. As I sat upon my swivel chair at the front of the raft, taking in the beauty of this stretch of river, I thought, "This is about as good as it gets." My patient guide Chris Russell set me up with a top-of-the-line fishing rod, took out the tangles in my line whenever they occurred, and netted my fish, then released them. Now this is fishing at its finest!

I have always refused to go whitewater rafting. George is the adventurous one, and his stories over the years have made me cautious. So when he told me we were all set to go rafting while we were at Northern Outdoors, I was apprehensive, to say the least.

I took the seat at the back of the boat, tightened my life vest, and took a leap of faith that my guide Mike McConnell knew what he was doing. And, of course, he did. Experiencing the rushing river for the first time was something I'll never forget. With my heart pounding, paddling hard, white water rushing toward me . . . I was exhilarated. This is outdoors in Maine at its best. I'd do it again in a heartbeat!

Our beautiful cabin for two at Northern Outdoors was set on a hill in back of the main lodge. It was about 20 degrees cooler in the shady woods. The cabins were immaculate, and include a well-equipped kitchen and an outdoor grill.

We ate our meals at the lodge for the two days we were there. The menu is mostly pub fare, which goes nicely with the on-premises brewery. After a morning of fishing out in the hot sun, we were really hungry. My chicken quesadilla included mush-rooms, roasted peppers, and lots of cheese. The delicious half-pound burgers are huge, served with what I deemed "the best sweet potato fries I've ever tasted"—crisp, and not at all greasy.

I had the dinner special that night—a spicy pasta dish that included both shrimp and chicken. I also tried the North-ern Salad; all kinds of fruit and vegetables made this a perfect choice for a hot evening.The portions here are huge. The service is great, and you have the option to dine inside or out, on the large outside deck.

George's choice that night was grilled sockeye salmon. (I'm sure he was remembering the salmon that gave him a fight earlier in the day.) He said the glaze was delicious.

The folks here really know how to accommodate the crowds of people they get arriving early in the morning for rafting. A couple of large groups arrived at breakfast, when we did, but everyone was served in a very short time. Their breakfast buffet includes crisp bacon, scrambled eggs, deep-fried potatoes (yum!), bagels, yogurt, granola, and lots of fresh fruit.

This was another of our fabulous mini-vacations—but a week here would be just the ticket to experience all that the region has to offer. And be sure to raft the gorge!

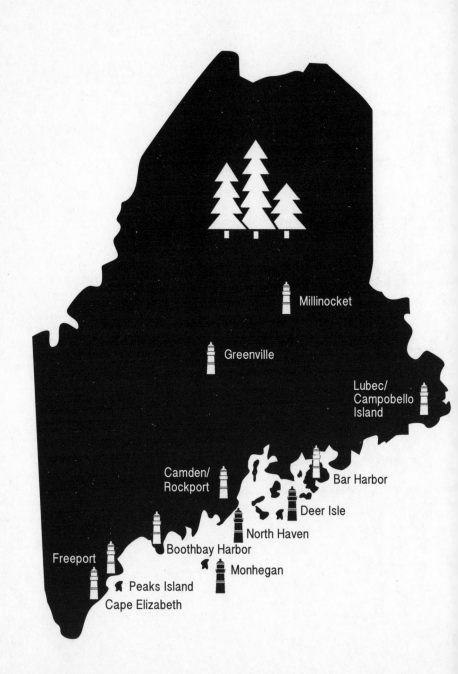

Millinocket

Greenville

Lubec/
Campobello
Island

Camden/
Rockport

Bar Harbor

Deer Isle

North Haven

Freeport

Boothbay Harbor

Monhegan

Peaks Island

Cape Elizabeth

Special Places
for Special Celebrations

Bar Harbor	The Bluenose Inn and The Looking Glass Restaurant
Boothbay Harbor	Spruce Point Inn
Camden	Camden Harbour Inn and Natalie's Restaurant
Cape Elizabeth	Inn by the Sea and Sea Glass Restaurant
Deer Isle	Pilgrim's Inn
Freeport	Harraseeket Inn and Maine Harvest Dining Room
Greenville	Appalachian Mountain Club's Gorman Chairback Camps
Lubec	Water Street Tavern
Campobello Island Canada	An Island Chalet
Millinocket	New England Outdoor Center, Twin Pine Camps, and River Driver's Restaurant
Monhegan Island	The Island Inn
North Haven	Nebo Lodge
Peaks Island	The Inn on Peaks Island
Rockport	Samoset Resort and La Bella Vita Ristorante

Special Places

You don't need a special occasion or celebration to enjoy these inns, restaurants, and activities, but when you do have something to celebrate and want a memorable experience, these are the places to go.

We once received a note from an eighty-year-old reader of our travel column after we'd written about a high-end coastal restaurant. She wrote, "Dear George and Linda: I really enjoy your travel columns, but there was no point in writing about ————, because no one can afford to eat there."

Well, you guessed it—the restaurant was packed that night. And while the lady was right, some of the best places are expensive. We all enjoy a splurge now and then, and a splurge in Maine costs a lot less than it does in many other places.

Surprisingly, many of these places are not at all expensive, especially for the high-quality experiences they deliver. We've given you a nice variety, from island inns to North Woods lodges. Time to celebrate!

Prices and hours of operation can change frequently, so we have not included them in the reviews in this book. Also, some places may close during the winter months. We have listed website addresses and telephone numbers and we encourage you use them to learn more information before planning to visit any of the places listed. We also encourage you to make reservations whenever possible, which can often make your travel experience more enjoyable.

Bar Harbor
The Bluenose Inn and
The Looking Glass Restaurant

The Bluenose Inn
90 Eden Street, Bar Harbor
General: (207) 288-3348
Reservations: (800) 445-4077
www.barharborhotel.com,

The Looking Glass Restaurant
50 Eden Street, Bar Harbor
(207) 288-5663
www.barharborrestaurant.com

Cuisine *AMERICAN / ITALIAN* | Minutes from *PORTLAND: 180, BANGOR: 75*

The Bluenose Inn focuses on providing the utmost in comfort and convenience for their guests. For example, there is an on-site, locked storage area for bicycles. Many come here to cycle the trials in Acadia National Park. The inn includes indoor and outdoor pools, a hot tub, fitness center, and steam room, and a wonderful spa.

Webster defines an inn as "a public house for the lodging and entertaining of travelers." That definition is insufficient for Bar Harbor's Bluenose Inn. Here's how we'd define the Bluenose: an elegant public house made of large luxurious rooms with ocean views, with a first-class hilltop restaurant featuring excellent food and entertainment options from indoor and outdoor pools to the piano player in the lounge, and heavenly spa treatments. Or you could just define the Bluenose as the "finest kind" of vacation. Until we started writing our travel column, we'd avoided Bar Harbor for thirty years. We were fearful that it was too crowded and touristy. We had a major attitude adjustment after our first weekend visit—we couldn't wait to go back!

The Bluenose Inn

Even as an admirer of the Lafayette family hotels, I was still unprepared for our experience at the Bluenose. The attention to detail and comfort is extraordinary—from thick towels to a handwritten welcome note, to shingled wastebaskets outside each building that match the siding. A lot of thought has been given to this special place.

Every member of the staff is super-friendly. No one—including maintenance staff and housekeepers—passed us without a greeting and an opportunity for conversation if we wished. Jim Ash, the manager and co-owner, was responsible for helping turn Rockland's Samoset Resort into a top-of-the-line destination, and we quickly discovered how—Jim's middle name must be "Hospitality."

We appreciated the chance to get to know Jim and his wife Diane on Friday night at The Looking Glass Restaurant, where they joined us for dinner. The view is unbelievable from this hilltop restaurant, and the food is equally as impressive. In fact, our dinner that night changed my dining habits. Neither Linda nor I like oysters, but when the chef sent out Oysters Rockefeller, we were astonished. They were fantastic! I also loved the Spicy Maine Crab Cakes so much that I had them for dinner on Friday night and then for breakfast on Saturday and Sunday as the base for my eggs Benedict.

For an entree I had "Halibut to Die For" (well, that's not what they called it, but it was). The Southwestern Grilled Fresh Halibut came with corn and black-bean cilantro salsa over green chili polenta—perfectly cooked and very tasty.

I'd also ordered up a side dish of another entree, the Lobster Mac & Cheese. Oh my gosh. In my LBL (Life Before Linda), my favorite dish was mac and cheese mixed with bits of grilled hot dogs. Well, lobster takes this dish to a whole new level.

They offer a clever tray of "mini $3 desserts," small portions that are just right to finish a meal. (I had a superb slice of carrot cake.)

Our suite on the fourth floor of the Mizzentop guest building was enormous with all the amenities you could ask for, including a beautifully decorated sitting room with comfortable seating, a gas fireplace, and a large flat-screen TV. The balcony, with a breathtaking view of the ocean and Bar Harbor's waterfront, was a great place for our morning coffee.

But a stay at the Bluenose goes beyond the gorgeous room. The grounds are immaculate, and the hospitality is first-class. Upon entering our room we found chilled champagne and an enticing fruit and cheese platter. The restaurant's view is breathtaking and their staff is extremely attentive and personable.

I don't eat much seafood, yet I loved the Oysters Rockefeller. The corn salsa served atop the crab cakes was spicy and delicious. My grilled beef tenderloin was perfectly cooked, and I'm still thinking about the amazing port wine sauce. This is dining at a high level (and not just because it's on a hilltop). Prices are reasonable for the quality of food and service. And there's one other thing that makes this restaurant uncommon. Even though it's the best fine dining, dress is casual— "Anything but bathing suits," said Jim.

We were lucky enough to stay two nights, and both nights we enjoyed the piano playing of Bill Trowell of Mariaville in the Great Room, which is filled with comfortable couches and chairs. Bill, who has been entertaining here for more than twenty-five years, took time to visit with every person in the room.

The spa staff is top-notch. Anita gave me a pedicure and my first manicure. My time with her flew by because she was so personable. Her niece Melissa runs the spa and gave George a massage he described as "amazing."

In the elevator on Saturday morning, a guest from Kentucky greeted us with a big grin and an unsolicited statement: "This is a wonderful place. I made my reservation in January, and I'm so glad I did!"

The Looking Glass Restaurant

I've lost track of how many times we've eaten breakfast at the Looking Glass, but I do know that I've had the Crab Cakes Benedict every single time. Our server, Tonya, tried to talk me into the Lobster Benedict, and although she made it sound enticing, I had been dreaming of the crab cakes and remained loyal to them.

Linda ordered a lighter version of eggs Benedict made with fresh spinach and raved about it. At one point, the friendly Tonya walked by our table singing. Now that's a happy staff member! And we were happy customers.

The Looking Glass is not open for lunch (drats!), but it does provide take-away lunches for inn guests who plan to enjoy a day at Acadia National Park, or elsewhere on Mount Desert Island. Guests make their lunch selections and hang the menu on the door of their room, specifying the time they'll pick up their lunch.

Still, it's the dinner menu that shines here. Jim was anxious for us to try the new vegan menu, and that was all the excuse we needed to return in September. Jim and his wife Diane joined us for dinner, as did my brother Gordon and his wife Janet.

Jim takes great interest in a restaurant's wine selections, and recommended an Adelsheim Pinot Noir from Oregon that he discovered at the annual Wine Expo in Boston. It was delicious.

As I glanced down the extensive menu, past entree favorites like the Seafood Medley and the Gorgonzola Stuffed Filet Mignon, I was sharply reminded by Linda that we were here to try the vegan dishes. I tried to order the regular tomato bisque, but Diane and Linda ordered the vegan version for me. Honestly, I didn't discover the difference until Linda told me.

Reluctantly, I ordered the Curry Vegetable Stew, somewhat mollified by the amazing rolls served with blueberry butter, olive oil, peppercorn, and rosemary. Linda chastised me for using the non-vegan butter. Yes, I was already falling off the vegan wagon.

But I must admit as I tasted my stew—composed of spinach, fresh vegetables, and tofu topped with toasted sesame seeds— it was delicious. The dish boasted coconut-milk broth, Thai-inspired curry, lots of vegetables, and it was very filling. I know our vegan readers are always looking for restaurants that offer creative meals, and this is definitely such a place.

It is commonplace to expect vegetarian options at restaurants today. A couple of decades ago, our parents' generation would have told you to "pick the meat out" of the dish they'd prepared, or have made you a salad. They would have worried frantically that you'd still be hungry.

Fast-forward and look at what is happening on today's food scene. Not only do many people eat mainly vegetarian dishes, but some are on gluten-free or vegan diets.

The Looking Glass Restaurant in Bar Harbor has recognized the trend and they now offer a number of gluten-free or vegan options. Their menu is exemplary due to the number of offerings that are gluten-free or vegan. A note on the top of the lengthy entree page explains that all items except mac and cheese could be ordered gluten-free. In addition, many appetizers are also gluten-free.

When we met with Jim and Diane Ash for lunch at the Looking Glass, Jim explained that he had worked with the chef to provide a new menu which included vegan items. I knew that I was about to learn how creative vegan dishes could be.

Sure enough, eight vegan appetizers were on the menu. The stuffed artichoke was very tempting, but I chose the Roasted Sweet Corn and Potato Chowder. They used coconut milk as a replacement for dairy. The chowder was full of potatoes and the fresh flavors of corn, roasted to crunchiness, but it was the intriguing herb flavor that had me guessing. It turned out to be marjoram, that made this soup extraordinary.

Entrees such as Potato and Cabbage Croquette and Mediterranean Stuffed Sweet Pepper were made with vegan cheese. Being a sucker for eggplant, I went with their unusual version of Eggplant Roulade. Grilled eggplant was stuffed with white-bean hummus, wild mushrooms, kale, and sweet potato. I also found summer squash, asparagus, and carrots in the crunchy vegetable filling. All of this was drizzled with an eighteen-year-old balsamic vinegar, adding another dimension of flavor. The portion size was big, and I enjoyed it reheated a couple of days later. I certainly didn't feel like I suffered by ordering the vegan option.

I'm not so sure we stayed on the vegan train the whole way, due to the fact that everyone ordered one of their mini desserts. My white chocolate mousse held a surprise of chocolate sauce at the bottom and was great. George's chocolate mousse was decadent, too. A mini dessert is the perfect solution to craving a little something sweet at the end of a meal.

Boothbay Harbor
Spruce Point Inn & 88 Restaurant

Spruce Point Inn
88 Grandview Avenue, Boothbay Harbor
(207) 633-4152

Reservations (Inn): (800) 553-0289
Reservations (Restaurant): (207) 350-1276
www.sprucepointinn.com

Cuisine AMERICAN | Minutes from PORTLAND: 80, BANGOR: 130

Oceanside massages as waves lapped the shore, dinner featuring amazing food and a gorgeous sunset, an amenity-filled suite overlooking the bay— our weekend visit to Spruce Point Inn was one we will never forget.

We visited Spruce Point Inn in the 1980s and found it in need of serious investment and renovations. Linda doesn't even remember our first stay here.

Until recently, we were unaware that two lifelong friends, Angelo DiGiulian and Joe Paolillo —who originally moved to Maine to work in the construction industry—had purchased the inn in 1991 with help from family members, and have been working ever since to make it one of Maine's top resorts. I was astonished at the transformation.

Angelo generously gave us a tour of the resort's extensive buildings and grounds including: conference facilities, outdoor and indoor dining rooms, and an outdoor pool. Guests have access to bikes, kayaks, forty-two acres of woodlands, and boat and shuttle-bus rides to town.

I was most impressed with the way they've totally renovated every cabin and building while keeping the historic look in tact. "A lot of what we did was uncover original woodwork and other features," Angelo said.

I also took note of the mackerel that guests caught right off the inn's dock. Guests can bring their catch to the chef and have them prepared for dinner. Should have brought my fishing rod!

Nostalgia compels many visits to the Spruce Point Inn, with multigenerational families returning year after year. As Angelo was giving us our tour, he noted that a guest who had been coming to the inn for thirty-five years was just checking out with grandchildren in tow. The average stay is three and a half days, but many come for seven to ten days. There's enough going on here to keep you busy for a week; that's for sure. Spruce Point Inn is a full-service destination resort, and while the busy and interesting town of Boothbay Harbor is nearby, we didn't even get there on this visit.

For our Friday night dinner at the Inn's 88 Restaurant, we were seated at the far end of the dining room surrounded by windows offering views of the ocean and sunset. It was white-tablecloth, linen-napkins, high-end dining at reasonable prices.

Ben, our server and an engineering student at the University of Maine, explained the dishes well. I will forever be grateful that he talked me into ordering the cedar-smoked Atlantic salmon. I had stopped ordering salmon after many disappointing bland presentations, but this version had a smoky taste with a wasabi-maple marinade that brought the right amount of heat to the fish.

My appetizer was a huge portion of Prince Edward Island mussels that were perfectly cooked and flavorful, with garden herbs, tomatoes, and Dijon mustard. Lamentably, with a lot of food ahead, I was only able to eat half of the mussels.

I managed to eat all of my large, perfectly prepared Caesar salad along with my salmon. For dessert, we tried something we've never had before: an orange liqueur sabayon—a perfect ending to this elegant meal.

There must be a reason that the Spruce Point Inn is the preferred lodging for Boothbay Harbor's Botanical Gardens (one of my favorite places in Maine). With lots of choices in the area, it can't be just location. I think it has to be the variety of accommodations offered at the inn in combination with great restaurant choices, quiet location, and wonderful service.

The rooms have been designed to keep the "coastal cottage feel." We stayed in the main inn where painted pine walls in the cooling colors of blue and white made me feel instantly relaxed.

I was impressed at the sheer size of the grounds—forty-two acres, including historical trails. There is an outdoor pool by the ocean and another by the spa. There's also a game lounge that is a popular spot for younger folks. The life-size outdoor chess set was pretty awesome, and the s'mores fireside station draws a crowd each night.

The Inn has a beautiful spa, and Angelo suggested that we try a couple's relaxation massage down at the waterfront. After checking in at the spa, we were driven down by the outdoor pool in a golf cart where a curtained tent-style structure sits near the shore. For one hour we listened to the sounds of the surf while getting massages. The massage was the most memorable experience I had all summer and one I daydreamed about during the following winter.

Our breakfast at Bogie's was great. This restaurant, with copper tabletops and an open feel, is more casual than 88. They offer a popular breakfast buffet, but I ordered off their menu. George (of course) had the buffet, including a lobster omelet.

I was intrigued by the Rustic Corned Beef Hash made with root vegetables. It was not at all your regular hash. Less salty and served with two sunny-side-up eggs on top, the taste of root vegetables shined through. This dish was a winner for me. The lunch menu looked very tempting as well.

The 88 Restaurant offers Maine coastal cuisine and fine dining in a beautiful setting. My roasted beet salad was served with baby pea shoots, local goat cheese, and a basil vinaigrette. Wow! We hadn't gotten too far into the meal when I realized that we needed to start bringing a stain stick with us on our culinary adventures. An acre of napkins wouldn't cover the stain on George's shirt. (For once, it wasn't me.)

The grilled Black Angus tenderloin was cooked to perfection. The beef was tender and moist, and when combined with its double-cream demi-glace . . . holy schmoley. Crispy potato strings and baby Brussels sprout leaves rounded out the meal, and made quite a presentation.

There's so much to do here; I especially regret not taking the boat tour around the bay. Next time!

Camden
Camden Harbour Inn and Natalie's Restaurant

83 Bayview Street, Camden
Inn: (800) 236-4266
Restaurant: (207) 236-7008
www.camdenharbourinn.com, www.nataliesrestaurant.com

Cuisine *AMERICAN* | Minutes from *PORTLAND: 105, BANGOR: 80*

Natalie's Restaurant offers a high-end, unforgettable dining experience that is the perfect way to cap off your stay. We can't wait to return.

Camden Harbour Inn

Elegance and sophistication combined with a friendly, relaxed informality put the Camden Harbour Inn at the top of our favorites list after a recent visit. Arriving at five p.m. during a heavy rainstorm, we were astonished when the bellhop dashed out to the parking lot with two umbrellas—a first for us. All of the rooms are named after Dutch islands. Our third-floor corner room labeled "Bonair," came complete with a flat-screen TV playing a video of deep blue Carribean sea with swimming fish and gurgling water.

Raymond Brunyanszki—who owns the inn with Oscar Verest—has put his personal touch on every aspect of this place since he and Oscar arrived in Camden in 2007. The word elegant doesn't really provide a satisfactory description of the design and the dozens of amenities that define the Camden Harbour Inn experience.

I've been a writer for forty years, and I just don't have the words to describe this place. I'd still be standing there at the window, staring at the view of Camden Harbor and Mount Battie, if Linda hadn't insisted we move along.

What does it mean to be truly pampered at an inn? The Camden Harbour Inn has figured this out. A fresh rose in your room, down bedding so fluffy you sink into it, a mattress that is a foot thick, not including the box spring (no kidding)! A stepstool might be required to reach the bed, but it provides the best night's sleep you can imagine.

After you return from dinner you'll find your room transformed: the shades have been drawn, bottles of water placed on bedside tables, and the screen saver on the TV has been switched from tropical fish to a virtual fire complete with crackling log sounds! A small box of chocolates sits by the pillows, and slippers are set by the bed.

The amenities continue: bath products from the UK, super-fluffy towels—I noticed the one I used before dinner had already been replaced when we returned to our room.

A claw-foot tub with European water taps sits in the large bathroom. Who can resist that? Choose between the "invigorating" bath gel, and the "stress-relieving" hydro-soak. The view of Camden Harbor from the tub will make you want to linger, trust me. Best view ever from a tub!

Each room has its own style with variations on traditional or contemporary themes. The inn's owners, Raymond and Oscar, redesigned and redecorated this inn when they bought it in 2007. It was Victorian, a style I've always found dark and foreboding, but the inn is now light and tastefully decorated throughout.

Natalie's Restaurant

There's a difference between eating and dining, both in the service and the food. Servers at dining establishments provide a high level of service, knowledge, and professionalism that is neither expected nor necessary at mere eating establishments. When we go out to eat, we're usually looking for tasty comfort food and lots of it. When we dine out, we expect food that is special.

At Natalie's both the food and the service are extraordinary. Shortly after being seated, I knocked my hardbound menu off the table onto the floor. I quickly retrieved it and set it back on the table. Our server, Patrick, dashed over, took it away, and returned with a new menu. After enjoying our first course, I set my napkin in my seat and visited the men's room (real towels!). When I returned, Patrick had taken my napkin and replaced it with a fresh, neatly folded one on a silver tray.

This level of service continued throughout our leisurely three-hour meal. We used enough utensils and dishes to take care of a couple dozen diners in most restaurants, yet we never felt rushed, and often didn't even notice our utensils had been changed until we reached for them.

The separate dining areas, a small bar near the entrance, the dim lighting, Italian music, white tablecloths topped by a single red rose, and the beautifully designed dishes all contributed to the intimate and sumptuous dining experience.

I began by examining the extensive wine list delighted to find our all-time favorite, Vino Nobile di Montepulciano from Avignonesi, a winery we have visited just outside Cortona, Italy.

Natalie's offers a three-course tasting menu, a five-course tasting menu, and a market-priced four-course lobster tasting feast. We ordered from the à la carte menu of four appetizers and five entrees. My wild mushroom soup included hen-of-the-woods mushrooms and was fabulous. And as a sportsman who loves all things deer, I ordered venison loin. It was smoked, a first for me, and came with a spaetzle that Patrick predicted would be the "best you'll ever have." He got that right. Yes, this was a cut above my own venison!

No matter what menu you choose, there are many additional elements that are included in the meal. I'll just say that I could have finish a gallon of the vichyssoise and enjoyed every single thing that graced our plates. There always seemed to be something coming from the kitchen for the entire three hours.

Our dining experience at Natalie's was spectacular. We ordered our favorite Italian wine while listening to Italian music. From the amuse-bouche of vichyssoise and chioggia beet cube with blue cheese, to my fall salad (served in an unusually shaped bowl), I was completely captivated. If we had salad bowls as gorgeous as theirs, we'd only have salad for dinner. And everything is delivered at exactly the right temperature.

The chef sent out hand-prepared gnocchi so pillow-soft that they melted in your mouth—better than any we've ever had, including in Italy. A cauliflower puree and thinly sliced wild matsutake mushrooms made this an incredible dish. It was fun to have these mushrooms (which I'd picked near our Mount Vernon home, and had been eating all week) prepared in such a different way.

I ordered beef tenderloin topped with horseradish crème fraîche. The dish also included tender boneless short ribs braised in Guinness beer. This, too, was excellent.

If you hate vegetables, come here and you'll be won over. My dish included a variety of colors of baby carrots, cubes of celeriac, and a turnip puree that was off the charts. There wasn't a potato in sight—nor did you need one. Veggies here are not a filler but a cause for celebration. The food portions were sufficient, but not so large that you were unable to enjoy all elements of a fine meal.

As the dining room prepared for sixty guests coming in from an evening concert at the Rockport Opera House, we moved to the lounge for our dessert. This was a cozy spot to enjoy the apple tart served with vanilla ice cream and a small glass of sauterne wine—a perfect ending to a perfect meal of incredible food and service. We spent just three hours dining, but the experience will live in our memory for years.

We are not big spenders. Our tip for this meal was more than we usually spend on an entire dinner but worth a lifetime memory like the one we'll always have from Natalie's. Eat here at least once in your life!

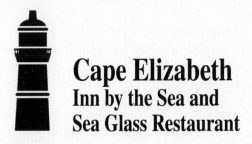

Cape Elizabeth
Inn by the Sea and
Sea Glass Restaurant

40 Bowery Beach Road, Cape Elizabeth
(207) 799-3134
www.innbythesea.com

Cuisine *AMERICAN* | Minutes from *PORTLAND: 8, BANGOR: 130*

We could live at Cape Elizabeth's Inn by the Sea, in a two-story suite with amazing ocean views, taking our meals at the world-class Sea Glass Restaurant, walking daily on Crescent Beach right in front of the Inn, bird-watching in the surrounding gardens and enjoying daily treatments in the luxurious spa. Whoops! Time to wake up! While none of us will ever live this dream, a visit to this fantasy location is possible.

Inn by the Sea

I am constantly astounded by the amazing places that are right under our noses. Sometimes I think that our out-of-state visitors know of more hidden gems in Maine than we do. That was certainly the case for me as we headed to Inn by the Sea.

The Inn by the Sea is a luxury hotel with incredible grounds and a view of the ocean from every room. The Inn was remodeled a few years ago. With a goal of preserving the environment, they became a Leadership in Energy and Environmental Design (LEED) Certified Green hotel.

Once you enter your room through a beautiful wooden door, you'll be transported to another world. Our spa suite had every amenity you could imagine—a spacious kitchenette, an extremely comfortable sitting area, a computer and work area, and a loft bedroom with an incredible ocean view. I suspect what will remain in my memory the longest is the jaw-dropping two-story windows that make up the entire back wall. (Push the button for the electric shades on that upper-story window if you don't want the sun to wake you.)

The vaulted ceiling makes this space seem enormous. Sliding-glass doors open to a small private deck overlooking the vast grounds and ocean. I felt like we were staying in an ultramodern apartment, not a hotel room.

You are bound to be impressed with the multi-room bathroom. The enormous shower included a bench and was large enough to count as a room. There was also a Jacuzzi bathtub opposite a wash area (extra amenities are stored in baskets on shelving below the sink). The toilet is in a room of its own.

We enjoyed every moment of our twenty-four-hour stay at Inn by the Sea. Every staff member is genuinely helpful, friendly, and professional. One of the servers described just how beautiful the gardens are here in the summer. Their gardener, Derrick Daly, created gardens of indigenous plant species over the past ten years.

Derrick told us Monday morning of three bluebirds he'd just spotted in the bushes outside. That's all it took for me to grab my binoculars, and get outside, where I saw a flock of ten bluebirds eating inkberries. Wow!

 Even the most gorgeous inn requires friendly professional staff to succeed, and the Inn by the Sea hits a home run. You'll never meet a more enthusiastic gardener than Derrick Daly—now Lin's friend for life. Our dinner server, Vanessa Helmick, was a fascinating young woman with her own interior design business. Everyone we met seemed to have all the time in the world to visit and make our stay special.

The inn's marketing director, Rauni Kew, is justifiably proud of the inn's significant commitment to the environment, something I especially appreciated as a sportsman/environmentalist.

From their partnership with Maine's Department of Inland Fisheries and Wildlife to create habitat for the endangered cottontail rabbit, to a long list of conservation strategies—including heating with biofuel—it's no wonder The Inn by the Sea is considered a top green hotel.

You'll want to enjoy the spa, but you'll also be tempted by the lengthy list of special activities offered, which includes a trip out lobstering where guests can catch their dinner.

For you folks who travel with a dog, the Inn reserves seventeen dog-friendly rooms and even offers a special doggy menu, which includes "Meat Roaff."

Sea Glass Restaurant

 What an excuse for gluttony! The Sea Glass Restaurant at Cape Elizabeth's lovely Inn by the Sea recently hosted an auction and five-course wine dinner to raise money for Alewive's Brook Farm, located just down the road from the inn. The Jordan family has worked the farm for three generations. More than eighty supporters gathered at the Sea Glass to bid on silent-auction items and enjoy dinner. The money raised that night was used to help build a new farm stand, including food processing equipment.

Sea Glass gets a lot of fresh seasonal produce from Jodie Jordan, as well as all of its lobsters. As Rauni Kew told us, "They are a terrific family, and deliver here to the inn as needed—sometimes seven days a week!"

It was not surprising that the Inn stepped up to help the Jordans. If an inn could have a conscience, this one would. The staff spends a lot of time and money on projects that help everything from monarch butterflies to cottontail rabbits. They also support Maine artists.

We love the Inn by the Sea and have enjoyed several fantastic dinners at the Sea Glass but this dinner may have been the best yet. Promptly at seven p.m., the chef sent out a spicy crab cake. And yes, it was spicy! But the grilled watermelon provided some coolness, and the avocado crema added even more taste. The Italian Lamberti Prosecco was paired well with this dish.

With her first bite of the second course (marinated beets and chilled lobster salad), Linda exclaimed, "Oh, I'm in heaven!"

"The lobster?" I inquired.

"Nope, the beets," she replied.

A bit later, she asked, "Who would ever think to scatter granola on a salad?"

Of course, I hadn't even noticed the granola, I was so focused on the chilled lobster.

As the superb wait staff brought new wineglasses and silverware, other servers delivered a beautiful plate of herb-grilled salmon.

The generous portion of salmon was nice and moist, with a tasty pomegranate reduction and a lot of braised cannellini beans that I especially enjoyed. The French Sacha Lichine single-blend rosé was another perfect pairing. I don't normally like rosé, but this was really good.

There was great conversation at our table where we were privileged to be joined by three generations of the Jordan family: Jodie, whose father purchased the farm in 1958; his daughter Caitlin, who now manages the farm; and his five-year-old great-nephew Sam. Sam had just helped the family plant potatoes for his third year! Yes, they start 'em young in the Jordan family.

If nothing more had come from the kitchen, we would have had a very fine dinner. But the fourth course was the best: slow-braised beef short ribs. This is one of my very favorite dishes anyway, but the Sea Glass has perfected it. A delicious mushroom sauce, grilled broccoli, and parsnip-potato latkes added a lot of flavor and texture to the dish. The ribs, easily cut with a fork, were tender and tasty, and the Alma Negra red blend wine from Argentina was my favorite of the night. Because we were staying at the Inn that evening, I was able to enjoy two glasses.

By the time the steamed lemon pudding dessert arrived, created by pastry chef Karen Voter, I was so sated that I forgot to take photos of it. Trust me—it was pretty! And it didn't remain on my plate for long.

I waddled the short walk up to our stunning two-story suite at the inn and dropped into a deep sleep. I may have dreamed of short ribs.

Alewive's Brook Farm is hardly my idea of a typical farm. Jodie is a lobsterman/farmer, and his daughter Caitlin runs the farm. It was a pleasure to be able to sit with them at this benefit dinner.

During our conversation, I was surprised to learn there are more farms in Cape Elizabeth than in my rural town of Mount Vernon. Caitlin named four full-time, year-round farms, and several more filling niche markets. I'd never thought of Cape as a farming community.

At the Inn by the Sea, the chef works his magic to turn these fresh products into delicious meals. I would have a hard time choosing between my favorite two dishes. The marinated beets and chilled lobster salad was outstanding. The vinegary red and yellow beets were well balanced with a granola dust for a touch of sweetness. Although not normally a lobster lover, I devoured the chilled lobster and arugula. All this was served atop a citrus crème fraîche. Bad news for George—not a speck left on my plate.

Young Sam was such a sport about all the fancy plated dishes put in front of him. He would try a bit of the different things and at one point asked, "Jodie, do you like that?" They placed a special order of chicken tenders for him, but more and more dishes arrived before he received them during the fourth course. Thank goodness the chef came through with Sam's chicken! His grin reached from ear to ear.

There was true Maine conversation throughout this special dinner. The talk bounced between fishing, golfing, farming, and great restaurants. I loved it. Great people, great food, and a great cause.

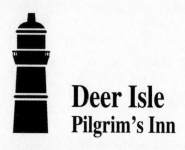

Deer Isle
Pilgrim's Inn

20 Main Street, Deer Isle
(888) 778-7505, (207) 348-6615
www.pilgrimsinn.com

Cuisine *AMERICAN* | Minutes from *PORTLAND: 180, BANGOR: 80*

Pilgrim's Inn is a place where history meets hospitality to give guests an unforgettable experience in island elegance. There's so much to do in Deer Isle, Blue Hill, and Stonington that you could spend week's exploring—at least, that's our new plan!

Pilgrim's Inn

Tina Oddleifson and her husband Tony Lawless own Pilgrim's Inn. They give previous owners much credit for the beautiful buildings, guest rooms, and restaurant. "There's a piece of every owner here," Tina said. And in the past decade they've made it their own.

The building was constructed in 1793 and turned into an inn in 1889. It closed during World War II, reopened in 1977, and was placed on the National Register of Historic Places a year later.

Extensive renovations have been made over the last thirty years, but the original features are still here, from wide pumpkin pine floorboards to tin ceiling. In our bedroom, I marveled at an old supporting timber, running from floor to ceiling, just below a modern recessed light. They've done a beautiful job of melding old and new.

Stunning art and interesting antiques decorate the buildings, and the two downstairs gathering rooms adjacent to the bar are wonderful places to linger with drinks.

We were in Ginny's Cottage 2, while our friends Rusty and Sue Atwood stayed in the adjacent Ginny's Cottage 1. Ginny was a lady who visited often, and now my goal is to get there enough times to find myself in George's Cottage 1.

Linda and I immediately felt right at home. I slept better than I had in weeks. The staff here makes you feel welcome. You might run into Tina and Tony anyplace, anytime—and they always have time to visit. The owners do it all here. We spotted Tina in the kitchen at dinner and out working in the gardens the next morning while Tony was mowing the lawn.

Saturday started with a scrumptious breakfast of fruit, juice, coffee, and blueberry pancakes—with real maple syrup, of course. Then we headed to Stonington. Tina had told me the area has the highest concentration of artists, artisans, and art galleries in Maine, and she wasn't kidding. We visited several that morning before grabbing a sandwich at a local shop and making a quick stop at **The Periwinkle**, where Candy Eaton offers a collection of wonderful kids' games and wooden toys, as well as books and art.

Tina and Tony provide great information about day trips, farms and local foods, galleries, and other opportunities in the area. They said their favorite nature trip is to the Barred Island Preserve, so we headed there in the afternoon. The hike to the island took only about twenty minutes. We crossed a gorgeous sand beach to wander around the island, where I got some great photos of an osprey.

Late afternoon found Rusty and me in heated games of Pétanque on the inn's court. He claimed to have never played, but I think he must have been secretly practicing, because he won every game. If the setting, beautiful grounds, the mill-pond, and the ocean across the road hadn't been so spectacular, I would have been despondent.

A visit here is like stepping back in time. The main Inn has pumpkin pine floors and features two eight-foot-wide original fireplaces—themselves incredible works of art. There are wonderful sitting areas in the common room and the library, a taproom where the bar is located, and a lovely dining room on the first floor. Guest rooms are on the upper floors.

More lodging choices include a large single cottage and the two adjoining cottages, where we stayed on our recent visit. The cottages are beautifully decorated with old fashioned decor. The large main room of our cottage held an antique corner cupboard, dining table and chairs to seat four, and a nice trunk used as a coffee table. The charming old lamps and wrought-iron chandelier give the cottage a distinct nineteenth century charm. Lots of windows keep the space light and cheery, with the pastel yellow walls lending a summery feel.

The small kitchen is fully stocked with equipment, providing everything needed to prepare meals. The bedroom is spacious, and its four-poster bed is so high that it requires a bit of a jump to get in! The bed was made with luxurious linens and was extremely comfortable.

The grounds here are massive, and you will find lots of spots to sit in one of the many wooden chairs placed about the yard to enjoy a book, a visit, or to just soak in the view. There is a full Pétanque court where the guys employed their competitiveness to enjoy some good games.

The deck connecting our two cottages was enormous. It made a great lunch spot under the umbrella of the patio set. The blooming bushes, well-tended flower gardens, and views of the water will make you want to linger outdoors.

The Pilgrim's Inn is just the place to enjoy the incredible scenery of Maine. All of this area was a new adventure for us. We headed to the small picturesque town of Stonington, where we strolled down Main Street. Isle Au Haut Boat Services is based here, and they offer trips to the island and Duck Harbor in Acadia National Park, sightseeing/lobster trips, and lighthouse cruises. Opportunities for another time!

Whale's Rib Tavern

 While there are several great places to eat in the area, the Whale's Rib Tavern in the Pilgrim's Inn offers the finest dining. From the moment we stepped inside, we fell in love with the dining room. With lots of windows and nicely spaced tables—it was a pleasant place to linger. No rush to turn over here.

Dinner was spectacular. A lengthy list of house cocktails, a good selection of Maine brews (including several that are gluten-free), and special wine list made our first dinner decision difficult. For wine, we opted for our tried-and-true Chianti, from La Striscia in Italy.

But the decisions grew tougher from there. Because Linda doesn't like—and doesn't cook—fish, I often order seafood when we visit restaurants. Two appetizers jumped out at me: local mussels steamed in white wine, garlic, and butter, and a seafood chowder. Concerned that the mussels might fill me up, I ordered the chowder.

Good choice. The chowder included large chunks of potato, haddock, and clams, was thick and nicely salted, and arrived in a beautiful bowl.

Perusing the list of entrees, I knew I was in trouble. I wanted them all! Thankfully, with four of us at the table and only six choices, I got to try four of them. Rusty saved the day by ordering the grilled rib eye. It would have been my choice, but I would have missed out on the seared sea scallops. That dish featured four huge fennel-dusted sea scallops with a tasty rosemary white-bean puree. The dark and salty olive tapenade and fried capers added flavor. I loved this dish.

Rusty's rib eye was delicious. The one-and-a-half-inch-thick steak was grilled in a cast-iron fry pan in canola oil for two minutes per side, with salt, pepper, and spices added, then placed in a 400-degree oven for eight minutes. It was a good thing he was seated opposite me at the table, out of reach, or I'd have eaten more of it!

I returned to our cottage stuffed and satisfied. But regular readers won't be surprised to learn that I mustered out the next morning for another great breakfast in the tavern: an omelet with red pepper, chive, cheddar, and sausage, served with sourdough bread.

Dinner at the Whale's Rib Tavern at the Pilgrim's Inn is not to be missed. The dining space, a former barn, sports barn-board walls and a top shelf full of wonderful antiques that circle the room. Wooden floors and small-paned windows add to the cozy atmosphere. At one point during our leisurely, early-summer dinner, a rainstorm passed through. Servers closed up the double screen doors and patrons happily relaxed into their meals, wishing to linger as long as possible.

Sue and I quickly settled on the arugula, fennel, grapefruit, and apple salad to begin our meal. It was a refreshingly light combination that went well with their Dijon champagne vinaigrette. Sue thoroughly enjoyed her entree of duck breast with wild rice, water chestnuts, and wilted greens. Beautifully presented, she commented that it had a great balance of textures.

Tina told us how lucky they are to be located within a "local farm mecca." She named two cheese makers, a farm raising organic chicken, and the presence of three local farmers' markets. "We have very fresh local ingredients readily available," she said.

When my eyes landed on the porchetta entree, I was transported back to a great day in Italy at a farmers' market in the town square. George got hungry while we made our way through the stalls, which sold everything from hardware and clothing to vegetables and cheese. Spotting a cart serving something on a bun that everyone seemed to be eating, we found out it was a porchetta sandwich. We split one sandwich and it was heavenly. I barely got two bites, but it was worth it.

Porchetta is pork shoulder and pork loin rolled together, filled with fennel, sage, and rosemary, and slowly roasted. The Tavern's version was moist and tender on the inside, had a crispy outside crust, and a rich herbal flavor. The dish was finished with creamy rosemary polenta and Swiss chard. What an amazing meal! It is an entree I have never noticed on a menu before, but will certainly be looking out for in the future.

I'd never heard of Boca Negra cake before, but it turns out it was made famous by Julia Child. This cake is intensely chocolate, made even more decadent by being served with a white chocolate ganache.

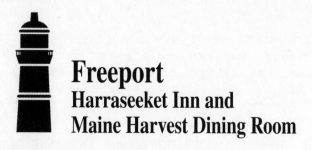

Freeport
Harraseeket Inn and
Maine Harvest Dining Room

162 Maine Street, Freeport
(800) 342-6423, (207) 865-9377
www.harraseeketinn.com

Cuisine *AMERICAN* | Minutes from *PORTLAND: 20, BANGOR: 100*

This classic country inn has eighty-four rooms and suites and nine extended-stay townhouses and it's within walking distance of L.L. Bean. Their two restaurants are the finest kind: the Maine Harvest Dining Room and the Broad Arrow Tavern. The Harraseeket offers amazing rooms, awesome dinners, and Maine's best brunch, and it's just a couple minutes' walk from Freeport's famous shopping area.

Five minutes after we entered the Thomas Moser Room at the Harraseeket Inn, I knew I loved the place. Our room was extraordinary, featuring fourteen stunningly beautiful pieces of furniture from Maine's own Thomas Moser. And every piece was available for purchase. Of course, we would have had to sell our house to afford it all, and then where would we put put it? But it sure was nice to luxuriate in their beautiful room for a weekend.

The Harraseeket delivers luxury along with fine dining at affordable prices. And the inn's package deals make it even more so. Families are especially welcomed during school vacation weeks.

But we were here to enjoy the Maine Harvest Game Festival in the Maine Harvest Dining Room. What a feast! Every year during the month of February, the inn features a special game menu. This year, executive chef Tony Mains created a new lineup of dishes. We were having difficulty making our choices until Tony came out to help us.

Given that he's an avid hunter, I was pretty sure he knew some good game recipes. And I was right. He recommended the antelope for me and the squab for Linda.

Our server, Carlos, has worked here since 1991. The staff seems to work here for long periods of time. We were pleasantly surprised to find one relatively new staffer, Jessica McCormick, a young lady who grew up in Readfield, and who came over to our table to say hi when she heard us mention that we live in neighboring Mount Vernon. Jessica is considered the new person in the dining room—even though she's been working here for three years.

I began dinner with the roasted Bandera quail, prepared with wilted greens, wild mushrooms, and Marsala wine sauce. It was a beautiful presentation. The quail was perfectly cooked, and I loved the mushrooms. There was no sauce left on my plate when Carlos cleared it.

While I've never hunted antelope, I have admired them sprinting across fields in the Western states and Saskatchewan. And I need to tell you that none of the animals on the menu here are wild—that would be illegal. These are farm-raised animals.

And the menu is not all meat. The vegetarian potpie was a popular item, and the seafood sampler delivered to a nearby table in a huge glass was a work of art. Boy, I wanted that! It looked soooo good. But I'd already ordered the antelope, and when it arrived, I quickly forgot about seafood. The chop was large and thick—more steak than chop, really—and served with mustard spaetzle, poached pear, broccolini, and mead-spiced bordelaise.

Linda, who does not often eat meat, kept demanding pieces of my steak; fortunately, there was plenty to share. In return, I got to nibble on the bones of her squab. Linda explained that spaetzle can be bland, but the mustard elevated it. Linda thought it must have also been pan-fried with the mustard.

Carlos delivered the dessert menu even as Linda was lecturing me about only ordering one. But I tricked her. This is one of the few restaurants that feature at-the-table preparation of some dishes, and there were four desserts on that list. I ordered the Jamaican bananas, without specifying for two, knowing that's what they'd prepare. And they did!

The flaming performance was very entertaining. The fresh-sliced bananas, Tia Maria, and Canadian pecans, flamed with Myers's dark rum and served on homemade vanilla ice cream—well, the description alone can still make me smile. I noticed Linda ate all of hers.

Back in our room, we enjoyed the wood fire. It reminded us of home. And we do feel at home at the Harraseeket—with or without the beautiful furniture.

Our room at The Harraseeket Inn, the Thomas Moser Room, was elegant and stylish. I love the sleek lines of design that are distinctly Thomas Moser. It reminds me of the simplicity of Shaker furniture, made with the same attention to detail. I also love the idea of hand-crafted furniture because it is such a work of art. The curved lines in some of the chairs give that modern feel, but this is furniture built to be used and to last for a lifetime.

The color scheme of our room was shades of gray with accents of brown. The room also featured luxurious draperies and wooden doors that slide on wrought-iron tracks. Our stylish white bathroom included a Jacuzzi tub, heat lamps, and plush towels.

A handwritten welcome note, bottle of wine, and a fruit and cheese plate welcomed us. The wood fireplace was set to go with the light of a match, which we did after enjoying a wonderful dinner.

I enjoyed meeting chef Tony Mains, and noticed that he checks in at all tables to talk to diners. You can almost hear the pride in his voice when he talks about being Harraseeket's executive chef. He stressed the effort the Grays take in using Maine products. I later read in the menu that they buy Maine products to support the Maine farmer, noting, "Maine is a special place, and we want to keep it that way."

An amuse-bouche of orange fennel crab salad on cucumber started this memorable meal. The fresh flavors made a delectable bite. A bread basket arrived, and underneath two varieties of house-made bread I discovered gold in the form of a cracker. The thin and crisp cracker with caraway seeds and salt was incredible, and was, of course, made here.

I selected the winter salad as a starter because I have never seen one remotely like it on a menu before. Freshly prepared chickpeas were combined with shaved fennel, black and green olives, and wheat berries. Diced roasted vegetables and a tahini dressing finished off the dish. It's not often that a salad has a tempting aroma, but this one certainly did! These were classic Mediterranean flavors highlighted in the best way possible.

Choices of entrees ranged from boar and buffalo to quail and seafood. There was also a vegetarian option of wild mushroom potpie. I selected the squab, something new for me, enhanced by a lingonberry-chipotle sauce. Each item on the plate has been given careful consideration, and the fresh spinach and nicely roasted baby potatoes were every bit as good as the main feature.

While the game menu is only served in February, the dinner menu here is always creative, and meals are memorable no matter the time of year.

The Harraseeket Inn offers pampering in all forms—afternoon tea, incredible food, and sincere service. It is the perfect place for a getaway.

Greenville
Appalachian Mountain Club's
Gorman Chairback Camps

Gorman Chairback Lodge & Cabins
1 Chairback Road, T7 R9, Greenville, Maine
Lodge: (207) 717-0270, Reservations: (207) 358-5187
www.outdoors.org/gorman

Northwoods Outfitters
5 Lily Bay Road, Greenville
(866) 223-1380
www.maineoutfitter.com

Minutes from *PORTLAND: 205, BANGOR: 100*

This is high-end comfort at reasonable prices—just the type of adventure that many of today's travelers seek. Good food and historic camps, in the heart of the hundred-mile wilderness. We rented equipment from Northwoods Outfitters in Greenville before arriving at the camps on a Friday night in March. It was a weekend to savor and remember—until we return for a summer adventure!

AMC Gorman Chairback Camps

When George said he'd like to stay at the Appalachian Mountain Club camps, I was intrigued. When he went on to explain that these are very comfortable camps, I was excited. But when he said people ski into and out of these camps, I was a bit panicked.

We used to cross-country ski when the kids were younger, mostly on Mount Vernon's snowmobile trails. Later, thanks to coach Steve DeAngelis and the Maranacook cross-country ski team, our kids, Josh and Hilary, really learned how to ski. George kept up with them for a while (until they left him far behind). I, on the other hand, continued to shuffle along on my skis and soon felt like a grandma far before my time! I decided I liked snowshoeing much more, and my skis gathered a decade's worth of dust.

My old skis with the three-pinned bindings now look like antiques. I couldn't even locate my poles and ski boots. So George reserved appropriate equipment for me in Greenville at **Northwoods Outfitters**. I credit those top-of-the-line skis and boots to my success in skiing that weekend, for sure!

After such a mild winter, it was great to see the perfect winter scene at Gorman Chairback. The older sporting camps sit on the edge of Long Lake, while four new camps are located just in back of them.

The Discovery School participants, some of whom had never skied or snowshoed before, were in good hands. Learn how to snowshoe and ski, visit a spectacularly beautiful area of the state, stay in comfortable camps, and have somebody cook for you! What a great way to have a winter adventure!

Our weekend was full of exercise. I knew that I needed to practiwce skiing (so that I could actually make the six-mile ski out). We were happy to find well-groomed trails. We didn't break any speed records, due to the breathtaking mountain views, and because George had to stop to examine every animal track, but it was fun. After enjoying our bag lunch back at camp, we went snowshoeing.

Everyone had spent a similarly busy day, and I don't think I've ever witnessed such thankful diners as those in the lodge that night. We were starving. We made short work of the many platters of turkey, potatoes, fresh green beans and carrots, and the best cornbread stuffing I've ever eaten.

After a hearty breakfast Sunday morning, we struck out on the epic ski back to the winter parking lot (in the summer, you can drive right to the camps). I was a bit worried that my trick knee wouldn't hold up, but it did, and I remembered how much I loved being out on those snowy trails in the woods. It was spring skiing that day—warm and absolutely perfect. And though I certainly felt it the next day, I knew I'd welcome the chance to do it again.

I didn't think we'd get to breakfast on our first morning, because the ground in front of the beautiful two million dollar lodge was covered with colorful white-winged crossbills, birds we hadn't seen all summer, and Linda insisted on watching and photographing them even as my stomach grumbled.

The food here is definitely worth the wait. Served family-style at breakfast and dinner, there is plenty for all. They pack lunches for you to enjoy wherever your daily adventure takes you.

Folks gather in front of a fire prior to meals, giving us a good chance to meet and visit with others, including a nurse from Portland, L.L. Bean guides from Bath and Monson, a family with teenagers from Cape Cod, a senior citizen from Boston, a Maine couple with a camp nearby in Brownville (their second visit here in a month), and friendly staff. This place offers outdoor opportunities without regard to your experience or expertise.

As darkness settled in on Friday night, we drove the thirteen miles from Greenville to the Gorman Chairback winter parking lot. Because we arrived late at night, we were transported to the camps in a coach behind a snowmobile—a rather wild ride.

On Saturday we skied above the lake in the morning, enjoying stunning views, and snowshoed along the enchanting Henderson Creek in the afternoon.

We opted for one of the new camps that includes indoor plumbing. The less-expensive older camps are also comfortable, but you must trudge to the lodge for toilets and showers. Been there, done that. We're into pampering now.

Gorman Chairback is one of three AMC camps in this area. The others are Little Lyford and Medawisla. I've stayed and fished at Little Lyford, catching thirty colorful wild brook trout on one hot sunny afternoon. Your entire stay can be at one of these camps, or you can travel from one to the other.

In addition to the above, here's what I loved: the toasty warm cabin on our arrival—thanks to the fire the staff had started for us; the smell of the pine walls; putting my feet up while reading on the couch; beating Linda at cribbage; the view across the lake toward the mountains; the amazing breakfast frittata in a huge cast-iron fry pan; and the old fishing photos on the walls (anglers really dressed up to fish in those days— and caught huge fish!).

On Sunday, we skied six miles to our Subaru (our longest ski ever), and then enjoyed the mud run the rest of the way to Greenville. The next day, almost a month early, AMC closed their camps because the roads were breaking up.

It was a carefree, in-the-woods weekend of relaxation, outdoor exercise, great meals, and a comfortable cabin—with just one problem: It went too quickly!

Northwoods Outfitters, Greenville

Mike Boutin is an experienced, highly respected, professional Maine guide, and his Greenville Northwoods Outfitters store has everything you need for a wilderness adventure, for purchase or rent.

His knowledgeable guides can show you moose to photograph or shoot, take you to the best fishing spots to catch native brook trout, get you into upland bird covers with a great dog, or give you a day to remember on a variety of equipment, from snowmobiles and ATVs to kayaks and canoes. Name it, and they do it!

This store is North Woods Central for information and advice, and we took advantage of that, asking a lot of questions about how to maximize our visit to the AMC camps. Mike actually called into the camps to double-check our instructions on Friday night—very helpful, as we were uncertain of road conditions.

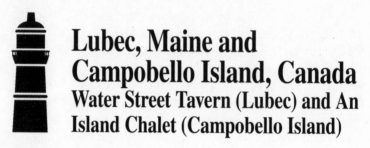

Lubec, Maine and Campobello Island, Canada
Water Street Tavern (Lubec) and An Island Chalet (Campobello Island)

Water Street Tavern Inn and B&B
12 Water Street, Lubec
(207) 733-2477
www.watersttavernandinn.com

Minutes from *PORTLAND: 245, BANGOR: 140*

An Island Chalet
115 Narrows Road
Campobello Island, New Brunswick, Canada
(506) 752-2971
www.anislandchalet.com

*DON'T FORGET YOUR PASSPORT!

If you can only visit one place in Maine this summer, make it Lubec (and Campobello Island, in Canada). We spend a lot of time there, as it's one of our favorite places on Earth. It's got lighthouses and lobster (and the world's best crabmeat), whales, gorgeous conservation lands along the ocean for hiking, world-class birding, kayaking, and fishing, Franklin and Eleanor Roosevelt's summer home, a two-thousand-acre international park, and even a great library that caters to visitors.

Sometimes things that seem insurmountable really aren't all that bad once you take a break and get refreshed. Lubec always refreshes me. Normally I am not ambitious. We left home on a Friday night to make the four-hour drive to Lubec.

A prior call to Mrs. Griffin at her home/shop in Edmunds made it possible to stop after hours and pick up some fresh crabmeat. (We stopped there again on the way home.) You don't need great cooking skills to make the most delectable crabmeat rolls ever with her super-fresh crabmeat.

We stayed at An Island Chalet on Campobello Island, which we discovered more than twelve years ago. Staying in Cabin 5 this time, meant we have officially stayed in every cabin there. It's like a home away from home to me. At our cabin, we could see the lights of Eastport, hear the ocean splashing the rocks and smell of the sea air. All this immediately eased my stress.

We scheduled this trip around George's brother Gordon and his niece Erica's run in the international marathon. On Saturday night, we reserved a table for seven at Lubec's Water Street Tavern as a pre-marathon celebration. Owner Jim Heyer was manning the bar that evening, and though he was busy, he stopped by several times. He was curious to see what we'd all ordered. When he saw I had a cup of Chef Theresa's black bean soup as my appetizer, he said, "That's an authentic Southern recipe. We're taking the Maine out of our chef—going to have her in the south soon!"

I haven't tasted a black bean soup that could come close to touching this one. Made with double-smoked bacon, a little sausage, beans, and tomatoes, this was one delicious soup! Just the ticket for a cool, foggy night.

I inevitably fall prey to the ravioli entree when I come here. Their wild mushroom ravioli is topped with fresh mushrooms and served in a Madeira cream sauce. It is consistently great, and I enjoy the leftovers just as much.

Nobody needed dessert, but our server convinced us that the Tall Three-Layer Chocolate Cake was sharable. I have never seen such a huge slice of cake! Jim told us this is the regular-size serving, and that he has seen individuals eat the whole thing, but that can't be often. The gigantic slice made its way around the table several times before we could clear the plate. Most of us took a single bite and passed it on, relishing the deep chocolate decadence. But soon we noticed that the cake slowed way down as it landed in front of Gordon or George. Hmmm . . . something about those Smith genes.

You can't beat an international weekend in Lubec, Maine, and Campobello Island, New Brunswick, Canada—especially if you are there for the international marathon, as we were.

My brother Gordon and his daughter Erica, along with friend Andy McClain, ran the marathon that began at West Quoddy Head Light, the prettiest place in Maine, and continued across the international bridge to East Quoddy Head Light on Campobello, and then returned to finish on Lubec's Water Street. Another friend, Katherine Ayers, ran the 10K from West Quoddy to Water Street.

That left Linda and I, along with Gordon's wife, Janet, as the cheering squad. It's a tough assignment, but we managed it. From our cabins at An Island Chalet, we walked to the hilly entrance to Campobello, where a large crowd cheered and shouted "Welcome to Canada!" as the racers passed.

Our next cheering assignment was at the finish line in Lubec, giving us ample time to check out and enjoy the shops and stalls that line the streets. The marathon drew more than 250 racers from thirty-four states, four Canadian provinces, and Peru, Iceland, Nicaragua, and Mexico. The 10K added 300 more. And every one of those runners got a huge round of applause and cheers as they approached the finish line.

Andy was the first of our group to finish, taking just over four hours. He said he took 44,723 strides. Ouch! Erica, who finished more than an hour ahead of her dad in last year's marathon here, ran with him this time as a special Father's Day gift.

They finished in five hours and fifteen minutes. Erica looked like she'd barely even started, while Gordon appeared near death. Well, not really. He amazed me, if not the others. Erica said the only problem was that every time he stopped for water, Gordon wanted to tell everyone about our history in Lubec and Campobello.

Our grandfather was from Campobello, our great-grandfather kept the light at West Quoddy Head Lighthouse for more than thirty years, our mother was born and raised in Lubec—oh, there was so much for Gordon to tell!

To say we feel at home here is a mighty big understatement, and I'm not exaggerating when I proclaim this the best place to vacation in Maine. Lots of ocean, uncrowded beaches, conservation lands, hiking trails, stunning scenery—and goose tongue greens (harvested on the edge of the ocean), a salty treat for dinner.

There are nice places to stay, from inns to cottages, but few as scenic and quiet as Rob and Diane Lahey's cabins at An Island Chalet. The cabins have full kitchens, a living room, and two bedrooms, one upstairs in a beautiful loft. On Campobello, we can fish from the docks, golf on the uncrowded island course, walk the trails and beaches in the two-thousand-acre international park, enjoy Franklin Delano Roosevelt's island home, go whale-watching with **Island Cruises**, and relax at our cabin, perched on the edge of the ocean.

In Lubec, we spend time at the great library, visit **Monica's Chocolates** (sometimes several times), walk the stunning oceanside trails from North Lubec to Cutler (the very best is at West Quoddy), and eat. Yes, there are some really good restaurants here.

Our favorite is Jim Heyer's Water Street Tavern, where the quality of the beer and wine is surpassed only by the food. I'm in a rut here, always starting with the mussels. And while I've broken out to enjoy the blackened haddock and barbecued ribs in the past, I always order, on our first visit each year, the Moqueca (Brazilian Seafood Stew). Jim calls it their "signature dish," and told me he'd had Brazilians visit who said it wasn't quite as good as it is in Brazil, but close.

The portion is huge, stuffed with seafood, and uniquely flavorful. I could only eat half of it, but Andy ate all of his. Guess he was storing up energy for the next day's marathon!

Our wine deserves special mention. Phantom by Bogle 2009, is described as "mysterious and hauntingly seductive, hard to get and harder to keep, a blend of old vine zinfandel, old vine mourvedre, and petite sirah," and "an allocated wine."

I asked Jim what that meant, and as always, when you ask him a question, you get a good story. This was his favorite wine when he and his wife lived in Florida. So when they opened the Tavern in Lubec, he called the company's vice president, found out that the entire state of Maine was allocated only twenty-six cases of this limited-production wine a year, and got himself a matching allocation of another twenty-six cases.

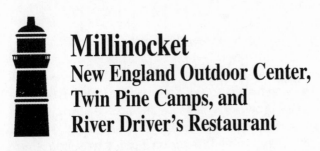

Millinocket
New England Outdoor Center, Twin Pine Camps, and River Driver's Restaurant

30 Twin Pines Road, Millinocket
General: (877) 331-0360
Reservations: (800) 634-7238
www.neoc.com

Cuisine *AMERICAN* | Minutes from *PORTLAND: 195, BANGOR: 90*

A recreational paradise in Maine's great North Woods, close to Baxter Park and its forty-seven mountains (including Mount Katahdin), the New England Outdoor Center (NEOC) has expanded from a small traditional sporting camp to a major destination that includes the region's best restaurant.

Matt Polstein is the perfect example of what it takes to succeed these days in the sporting camp business. Matt has renovated most of the old cabins that were part of Twin Pine Camps, constructed new cabins and luxurious three-bedroom houses, added a superb restaurant, partnered with conservation groups to protect surrounding lands, and added outdoor recreation activities to the traditional pursuits of hunting and fishing.

For example, as rafting, one of his principal businesses, declined, he added birding, biking, and other outdoor activities. And he added "floating" the West Branch of the Penobscot River, a half-day trip, for those who are less adventurous and don't want to devote an entire day to whitewater rafting. Passive activities like moose watching are also featured in the summer and early fall.

When we were there recently, it was clear that the New England Outdoor Center is a major destination for snowmobilers. While Matt rents snowmobiles, many of his guests arrive with huge trailers full of their own. Some bring two for each member of their party, in case one breaks down!

Of course, it doesn't hurt that NEOC sits on the shore of Millinocket Lake, just eight miles on a paved road from the town of Millinocket, with gorgeous views of Mount Katahdin and access to the entire North Woods. It is also just minutes from one of my favorite rivers, the West Branch of the Penobscot, with its fabulous fishing, canoeing, kayaking, and rafting.

I've visited great lodges in Montana, Alaska, and Quebec, and Twin Pine Camps ranks with the best. And, oh yeah, the food is worthy of the Portland dining scene—but it comes with better scenery!

In 2012, Linda and I stayed in one of Matt's new environmentally friendly houses (he insists they're cabins, but they are huge), so this time we asked for one of the original Twin Pine cabins. All of the cabins, old and new, have full kitchens and lots of beds. The largest cabin sleeps fourteen people. Little Mud Cabin was down on the lake with stunning views of Katahdin—well, there would have been if it wasn't snowing most of the time we were there!

We actually drove up to Millinocket in a blizzard, and that was adventure enough for that day, so even before we settled into our camp, we visited the River Driver's Restaurant for lunch. Matt moved his popular restaurant from east of Millinocket to Twin Pine Camps a few years ago. I loved it in the old location, but here, it's an impressive two-story building with conference and celebration spaces, and huge windows offering views of the lake and Mount Katahdin.

As impressive as the location and view are, the food is even better. After that drive, I was ready for a beer, and was delighted to find one of my favorites, Allagash Black, on the menu. It went very well with my pulled-pork sandwich.

The fries are large and crispy and so plentiful, and I actually couldn't eat all of them.

As much as I enjoyed my sandwich, I must admit Linda's Cajun blackened chicken breast was even better. It was very spicy. At one point, she exclaimed, "My mouth is on fire—in a good way!" When I asked her what would be a bad way, she said, "That time you ate the hot cherry pepper." Well, yes, but that was a mistake.

We settled into our cabin for the afternoon, glad to be inside while the wind-whipped snow flashed past our windows, until we bundled up for the short walk to the restaurant for dinner. Before ordering, I walked around, taking photos and admiring the artwork and other decorations.

I love their crab-cake appetizer, so I convinced Linda to share that. They were delicious, seared in butter with fresh herbs and lemon zest, and covered by a peppered Limoncello remoulade. I've never forgotten the crab-stuffed haddock I had here in 2012, so I was ecstatic to see that it's still on the menu. And it's still fantastic, topped with a lobster claw and delicious lemon caper cream sauce.

The crispy carrots were a tasty surprise. When Linda asked if I knew why I loved them, I didn't know the answer. "They are glazed in honey and cooked in butter," she explained. No wonder! We both fondly remembered the chocolate torte dessert and shared that. It was sooo good. We lingered in the busy restaurant until 9:30 p.m., enjoying dinner, and feeling blessed. And eleven hours later, we were back for breakfast!

But after that, Linda insisted on some exercise, so we put on our snowshoes and hiked Matt's ski/snowshoe trail up on the ridge. The woods were far less windy, and we enjoyed a nice snowshoe for about an hour before packing up and heading home.

For our most recent visit to Twin Pines, we stayed in one of the older cabins rather than in one of the new "green" guesthouses as we had done in previous trips. They were excellent, but we wanted to try something different.

Twin Pines has been updating some of their older cabins, and Little Mud, were we stayed, had just been remodeled. They have installed new interior walls and half walls to enclose sleeping spaces. Our camp has two full beds and one set of bunks, so it sleeps six. New cabinets are filled with everything you'd need to cook with—from dishes and silverware for six to a coffeemaker, microwave, and toaster.

The weather this trip wasn't as cooperative as last time, but even with snow and whipping winds, people were enjoying an outdoor winter experience. This is the home base of the New England Outdoor Center (NEOC). Trails for skiing, snowshoeing, and snowmobiling are well kept and easily accessible. I even got George to go snowshoeing despite the winds and blowing snow. The trails are beautiful, and it was very pleasant in the woods out of the wind. He admitted that it was great once we got out there. An hour of exercise in winter beauty can really help relieve cabin fever.

River Driver's Restaurant is the place to eat up here. Their food is consistently great. For lunch I loved the Twin Pine sandwich—Cajun blackened chicken, bacon, Swiss, tomato, and jalapeno ranch dressing. The Cajun spices were cooled by the dressing and accented with the salty bacon. I enjoyed every bite.

During our evening meal we sat in the more-private section, which has a lovely feel. One wall is made up of wine housed in a custom-made rack, which is as pretty as a sculpture. Copper-topped tables, soft lighting, and windows facing Katahdin add to the ambience here.

I ordered one of the evening specials—Steak Caprese. An expertly cooked sirloin was topped with basil and mozzarella, and served with mashed potato and glazed carrots (caramelized and yummy). The servings are generous, so I enjoyed it just as much as leftovers a few days later.

We agreed to split their flourless chocolate torte, which was decadent and delicious. Served with vanilla bean ice cream and a chocolate drizzle, this one had a gooey filling and a crunchy chocolate crust. It was "over the moon" good!

And to round out the dining experience, we enjoyed breakfast before we headed home. My NEOC Egg Scramble held spinach, mushrooms, and Swiss cheese. It's made with three eggs, and they couldn't really cut it down to two as I requested, so it was an enormous breakfast. When our server delivered this she said, "You probably won't need lunch!" And I certainly didn't, but it was great reheated the next day. I'd be remiss if I didn't mention the amazing three-potato home fries. The combination of sweet, red, and white potatoes is as pretty as it is delicious.

The Twin Pine Camps are prime accommodations in any season. It's a short drive to Baxter State Park and all the outdoor experiences the park offers, spring through fall. New England Outdoor Center's whitewater rafting, leisurely float trips, and snowmobiling adventures, make it a sure bet for your lake and woods vacation.

Monhegan Island
The Island Inn

The Island Inn
1 Ocean Avenue
Mohegan Island
(207) 596-0371
www.islandinnmonhegan.com

Cuisine *AMERICAN* | Minutes from *PORTLAND: 76, BANGOR: 120 (+90 MINUTE FERRY RIDE)*

The hotel has thirty-two rooms and suites. A great buffet and cooked-to-order breakfast is included with the room. Please note that it is BYOB for dinner. There are a couple of places to buy wine and beer on the island, including the Barnacle Cafe and Bakery, which the hotel owns and operates. Monhegan Boat Line (207-372-8848; monheganboat.com) in Port Clyde operates a ferry and provides transportion to the island.

The Island Inn

Two years ago, after our annual Mother's Day birding adventure weekend on Monhegan ended we heading back to the mainland on the Barstows' Monhegan Boat Line, when we struck up a conversation with Michael Brassard and Jayne Morency on the upper deck. Turns out the had just purchased Monhegan's Island Inn, and after a great talk, they invited us back to the island to stay at their inn.

In May, we stay at **Shining Sails Bed & Breakfast** on the island. We love Shining Sales and I would spend the entire month of May there if I could. The bird watching is fantastic during May.

However, we decided we'd also like to visit in the fall, as the birds headed south. We were astonished to discover that The Island Inn was completely booked that last weekend in September. We were lucky when we got the last available room for the third weekend in September.

And now we know why—it's a great place to stay, and an even better place to dine. Michael was concerned that our room was small, with twin beds and a sink, and a shared bathroom across the hall. But we're Mainers. We make do. The ocean view from our second-story room was spectacular, and the room was plenty comfortable. We actually spent very little time in it.

We enjoyed all the first-floor public rooms, one with a fireplace that warmed us after a cool afternoon of birding around the island. On Sunday morning, I spent a couple of hours enjoying a rocking chair on the deck, overlooking the open ocean, while Linda did more birding (yes, she is obsessive about this).

The Island Inn is stunning, sitting atop the hill above the waterfront and boat landing, and the staff is super-friendly. So, too, were the guests—including an Audubon tour group visiting to see the fall migration of birds.

When we visit Monhegan in the spring, most places are not yet open, so it was fun to see the island bustling in September. We especially enjoyed lunch at **The Barnacle**, and a microbrew at the Island's fabulous brewery, **Monhegan Brewing Company**. Winter Works, featuring the work of local year-round artists and craftspeople, is spectacular, and we enjoyed visiting with Cynthia Charles, who was minding the store that day. Cynthia grew up in Wayne, and we discovered that we have several friends in common.

It was a rough and windy trip to the island on the ferry. Despite the rain and wind, we sat outside on the upper deck, where the air helped us avoid seasickness.

The inn's dining room is elegant, decorated with spectacular art, with seating for sixty diners. We quickly claimed a table by the window with an ocean view. Tables are close enough together that you can visit with others, if you wish, and we did.

We all laughed when we noticed that at each of the four tables in our section, the man had claimed the inside seating, a nice bench with pillows.

Our server Ashley helped us with our dinner selections. At my request, she brought a taste (about half a regular serving) of New England–style clam chowder, which was good, with lots of chunks of clams and a salty, creamy broth. Showing remarkable restraint, I did not eat all of the bread that came with our appetizers.

The bacon-wrapped scallops were not only very beautifully presented, but each scallop was perfectly seared and wrapped in a crispy delicious piece of bacon. The maple glaze was tasty, and the sweet roasted corn made for a nice combination of flavors and textures. My only problem with this appetizer was that Linda loved it too, so I didn't get to eat it all.

It's BYOB here, so we'd purchased a bottle of Stemmari Nero D'Avola at the island's small grocery store, L. Brackett & Son.

The chef was Martha MacDonald, a native of the small fishing village of Antigonish, Nova Scotia. She earned a culinary degree at Nova Scotia Community College, Strait Area Campus, winning the 2011 USA Pears "Pear Excellence" Canadian competition in Montreal. She lived and worked in Portland before coming to the Island Inn.

Chef MacDonald's list of entrees was impressive, making my choice especially difficult. Seafood pappardelle, prosciutto-wrapped seared Scottish salmon, the filet mignon, maybe the Monhegan seafood stew? Oh, what a tough decision! I opted for the evening special of grilled halibut, with pineapple salsa. The pineapple added a nice flavor to the moist halibut, with just a tiny bit of fresh lemon squeezed over the top.

At seven p.m., partway through our meal, the sun set, leaving the island shrouded in darkness outside our window. Conversations were flowing all over the restaurant, about lodging, food, the brewery, famous people that spend time here, and birds (of course!). Wherever we went on the island, people had a camera, binoculars, or both.

All of the couples we enjoyed talking with at nearby tables were "from away." One had visited Acadia National Park prior to spending three days on Monhegan. "We were researching classic Maine islands," said the young lady. Two tables down, an older lady exclaimed, "We love the off-season here." They were on the island for two weeks, renting a cottage.

I should not have had dessert, but I was intrigued by the chocolate carrageen traditional "firm pudding"—made using MacDonald's grandmother's recipe—with seaweed she gathers from Monhegan's Lobster Cove. It was unique, for sure, with lots of chocolate chips, blueberries, and whipped cream, along with a raspberry sauce—fortunately, nice and light.

We opted for the 12:30 p.m. return ferry on Sunday, allowing us to enjoy the inn's popular Sunday brunch, and spend a couple of extra hours on the island. In addition to the breakfast buffet items—including a wonderful blueberry-stuffed French toast, along with bacon, sausage, muffins and biscuits, and, oh yeah, healthy fruit and three kinds of juice, plus coffee—I also ordered lobster scrambled eggs. Yum! I could barely make it from the table to the porch, where I spent two hours reading and waiting for the ferry.

The ride back was wonderful—calm waters, hot sun. Now we are dreaming of our return in the spring!

North Haven
Nebo Lodge

Nebo Lodge
11 Mullins Lane, North Haven
(207) 867-2007
www.nebolodge.com

Cuisine *AMERICAN* | Minutes from *PORTLAND: 100, BANGOR: 95 (+70 MINUTE FERRY RIDE)*

Maine islands have become favorite getaway locations for us, and thanks to Nebo Lodge, North Haven just rose to the top of the list! With just a short ferry ride from Rockland, you'll soon be enjoying the quiet charm of this very special place. The Maine State Ferry Service (207-596-5400 or maine.gov/mdot/ferry/) provides regular service to the island.

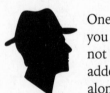

One thing we love about Maine's islands is that you can walk down the middle of the street and not worry about getting run over. Our recent trip added North Haven to our favorite islands list, along with Peaks and Monhegan. These are places where you start to relax with the first step off the ferry, and enjoy surprisingly good food, comfortable lodging, and awesome views. If you've never vacationed on a Maine island, do it this year!

If you want to stay at Nebo Lodge, make your reservation early (they start taking them in January). The Lodge is owned by US Congresswoman Chellie Pingree and managed by her daughter Hannah, a former Speaker of the Maine House of Representatives.

We tried to book a room from the Lodge's opening in early May through September, but my attempts failed—because the Lodge was fully booked all spring, summer, and fall!

We finally made it, getting a room two weeks before they closed for the season at the end of October. It was worth the wait, and we were actually lucky to get that room, because Liz, the Lodge's innkeeper, was getting married that weekend, and the island was packed with celebrants.

Our room, located in the historic Lodge's annex, was handicapped-accessible, comfortable, and spacious. The main building has eight rooms—four with private baths and four with shared baths. Chellie and some friends purchased the historic inn in 2005, at that time a private residence, and substantially renovated it, maintaining much of the old beauty of the building and reopening it as an inn.

The staff is super-friendly and eager to make your stay remarkable. Hannah even loaned us a truck so we could drive around the island's thirty miles of roads and enjoy the stunning views. The inn also has bikes for exploring the island.

After our tour of the island and a nice nap, we were ready for dinner. Having read many reviews of chef Amanda Hallowell's cuisine, we knew we were in for a treat. The Lodge's front room and bar were jammed with locals and visitors gathered for the next day's wedding. The interior room, saved for those with reservations, was nearly full when we arrived at seven p.m. As soon as we were seated, I started swooning over the Italian background music, until Linda informed me it was French!

When I asked our server, Hannah, the island's pre-K teacher, what her favorite "First Tastes" item is, she said the roasted squash salad. So I ordered it. The roasted squash was the star, and the wonderful variety of greens, crispy bacon, onions, and cheese all added flavor to the lightly dressed dish. A good choice, indeed.

While I appreciated the "Light Suppers" menu, featuring interesting preparations of tacos, burgers, and pizza (something you don't often see in fine dining restaurants, and an obvious tip of the chef's hat to those who prefer less-expensive dinner options but still want creative food), I wanted Amanda's best, so I focused on "Main Courses."

My choices included: A couple of pan-seared rosemary-marinated steaks; a bouillabaisse with Maine shrimp, cod, mussels, tomatoes, chili peppers, garlic, white wine, and thyme; an organic duck confit with herby lentils, roasted baby carrots, and a marmalade glaze; or Maine lobster bohemienne in cream sauce with parsleyed fingerling potatoes and a French roll.

After a lot of dithering, I chose the duck confit. The duck was soft and tender, the black lentils, tasty, the carrots, crispy, the marmalade sauce, not too sweet or overpowering. Delightful. While I begged for the black pepper affogato for dessert, Linda said no, afraid the espresso topping would keep me up all night. So we shared a couple scoops of ice cream. Unfortunately, eager to grab the last spoonful, I dribbled it down my shirt and onto my pants.

 How is it possible to grow up in Maine and never have visited either Vinalhaven or North Haven islands in my sixty years? Quite possibly, I am not the only one, so let me try to paint a picture of North Haven for you.

We began this adventure on the ferry. Be aware that there are separate tickets for the trip to North Haven and the return trip to Rockland. When George returned with two tickets in his hand, I was glad I inquired how much the two tickets cost. He got a funny look on his face and said, "Oh, I think I only bought tickets for one of us." Otherwise, I might have been left on the mainland!

Located just twelve miles off the coast of Rockland, this eight-mile-long island sits so close to its neighbor, Vinalhaven, that it looks like you could swim across the thoroughfare.

Approaching the ferry landing, my first impression was of a lobstering community, from bays filled with lobster boats. But the mix of pleasure boats let us know that this is a vacation destination for many.

While walking the island streets, we discovered **Waterman's Community Center**, where kids and adults were playing card and board games in the front room. A pre-K classroom is located at the back of the first floor, beyond the cafe.

The importance of community is crystal-clear here. Everyone says hello as you walk by, and every single driver waved at us as we drove the roads. It's part of the culture here, making me feel as if I was welcomed into their world, rather than intruding. The views of open fields, rural living, and the ocean are stunning. A short climb up Ames Nob revealed breathtaking views of the Camden Hills, Vinalhaven, and the open ocean. We discovered many small beaches, some lined with shells, and most open to the public.

Nebo Lodge's restaurant is causing quite a stir and has been featured in regional and national magazines. North Haven native Amanda Hallowell is the chef here, and prefers to call herself a cook. I'm not sure I agree with that.

Everything we tried at dinner and breakfast the following morning was delicious, beautifully presented, and featured the freshest locally grown ingredients. At dinner, I was so glad I'd ordered the cream of celeriac soup. Smooth doesn't begin to describe the texture. The subtle flavor of celery accented with the nutmeg made this the best soup I've tasted in a very long time. It's a simple dish, yet one that will linger in my memory.

This is a lovely restaurant, simply decorated and inviting with antique tablecloths and china. At night the soft lighting enhanced by candlelight bounces off the cream-colored walls and wood ceiling to create a cozy atmosphere.

I chose the island-raised beef dish—rosemary-grilled rib-eye steak served with a bright Italian salsa. The perfectly cooked tender beef was extraordinary, and the herbed salsa was so flavorful. Truffled french fries accompanied the dish—an unusual and tasty presentation. George was ready to try all the delectable desserts, but I talked him into splitting their house-made ice cream. Two scoops gave us a chance to try ginger and a malted chocolate ice cream. Wow! I absolutely loved the ginger.

A continental breakfast is included with the room, featuring freshly baked muffins or scones, yogurt, cereals, juice, and Rock City coffee. Made-to-order breakfast choices are also available. My farmer's egg scramble included Swiss chard, red peppers, goat cheese—a nice combination. George's baked egg dish with fresh herbs, cream, and Parmigiano-Reggiano was tasty as well.

After breakfast Sunday morning, we sat in the warm sun on the Lodge's porch. We talked about the more than 350 Maine islands that once hosted year-round communities. Today, only 15 islands are occupied year-round. The 350 year-round residents of North Haven maintain a vibrant community, including the state's smallest K–12 school of 62 students. We felt very blessed to have experienced this community, if only for twenty-four hours.

Peaks Island
The Inn on Peaks Island

33 Island Avenue
Peaks Island
(207) 766-5100
www.innonpeaks.com

Minutes from *PORTLAND: 0, BANGOR: 120 (+15 MINUTE FERRY RIDE)*

Only a fifteen-minute ferry ride from Portland, the island offers a quiet, relaxing experience featuring wonderful accommodations, great food, stunning scenery, and friendly people. Casco Bay Lines Ferry (207-774-7871; www.cascobaylines.com) provides regular service to the island.

We visited Peaks Island on a Memorial Day weekend. We birded, feasted, luxuriated in our gorgeous room, sunned ourselves on the deck, and hiked all over the island, including its extensive conservation areas.

And we got one surprise treat: a wonderful parade celebrating Memorial Day (two days early) that we watched from our room's outside deck. We especially loved Portland's Mahoney Middle School band. Awesome job, kids!

Rooms at the inn feature bright colors, lots of amenities, comfortable chairs and couches, a gas fireplace, large refrigerator, and a sooo-soft bed.

The inn's food rises well above pub fare, and, unlike our first visit, we were able to sit outside for our meals. Imagine sitting there, enjoying a Shipyard brew or glass of wine and a very tasty appetizer, while watching the sun set over Portland across the water. Wow!

Two dinners and one lunch gave us a good opportunity to experience much of the inn's menu. The bar was packed with islanders and somewhat rowdy on Friday night, so we settled into a table in the quieter dining room, where folks at the closest tables shared laughter and news about families, boats, and homes.

"What's new in Philly?" asked one.

"Temperature's going to be ninety-five there tomorrow," came the answer. No matter if they are permanent residents or summer folks, everyone feels at home here, including us.

My seafood Puttanesca that night was delicious, featuring a hearty tomato sauce with kalamata olives, capers, calamari, mussels, and Maine shrimp served over fettuccine. I loved it. We'd had hot and spicy chicken wings with a great ranch sauce about four p.m., starting our own version of a progressive dinner.

After enjoying our Friday-night meal from seven to nine p.m., we continued our progressive dinner theme, taking our dessert to our room to enjoy on the deck.

On our Saturday-morning walk around the island, we spotted three dozen species of birds. The benches along the oceanside drive are really nice, and we sat for a while, enjoying the surf and the hot sun while scouring the water for birds.

Cecilia, our exceptional server for most of the weekend, and a student at the University of Southern Maine, arrived by ferry in time to serve our lunch. I really overdid it, ordering the special fried-clam appetizer and the fish taco. Portions here are huge, and I felt compelled to eat it all. The clams were spectacular, with a homemade tartar sauce that had some zing to it. The taco was imaginative, featuring haddock with a house taco seasoning, lettuce, chimichurri sauce, and a mango black bean salsa, served in a thick folded flatbread. Very good.

Hard to believe, but I was ready to eat again that night (after Linda forced me to take another long hike around the island on Saturday afternoon). We ended the walk with a cold lemonade, sitting in the shade on a bench in the town square.

At dinner that night, Andrew, the bartender, made a nice white-towel presentation of our Cigar Box Malbec, 2011 Reserve, and we lingered over our dinner, enjoying visits with several of the inn's staff members.

The starter cup of clam chowder was really good, and I loved the fried ale-battered haddock—three generous pieces of fish, lightly crusted, with that same tartar sauce that I enjoyed at lunch.

Our ferry ride over on Friday night was in "pea soup" fog. The crowd getting off the boat moved with purpose, some with pushcarts filled with groceries, or loaded with flowers for planting.

When I awoke on Saturday morning to clear blue skies, I urged George to get moving so we could see some birds. Equipped with our binoculars and a bird book, we were off for a hike. We'd only made it to the side of the inn when we encountered birds everywhere! In a very short time we'd spotted cardinals, several varieties of warblers, and more. One resident came out of his house, curious about what birds we were seeing. When we told him what he had right in his own trees, he was pretty surprised. We eventually hiked a shore route into a conservation area that was filled with birds. Just as we suspected, this is a birder's paradise.

On this beautiful 80-degree day, almost everyone was either out walking or jogging in the morning. Around noon-time we started noticing a change in activities, to biking or gardening. The people here seem to live outside as much as possible.

At the inn, our "Chebeague Island" room was on the front of the building, affording us a view of the water and Portland's tall buildings beyond. An open main room features a couch, fireplace, and bed. There's a vaulted pine ceiling on the front half of the room. The outside deck overlooks the ocean and the square where people exit the ferry.

The rooms here are neat and tidy, without any clutter. The pale yellow walls and white woodwork make this room bright and cheery, but it's the brightly painted furniture that gives this room a decidedly island feel.

We noticed there were always people dining, no matter the time of day or night. Many took advantage of the great weather and were eating outside. A nice lunch item was the Brewer's Choice chicken sandwich: golden-fried chicken with prosciutto, beer cheddar, and a cherry pepper aioli. Yum!

The risotto-stuffed portabella for dinner was also special. Creamy risotto filled the earthy mushrooms topped with a crumb crust. A meal like this while watching a huge red sun disappearing behind the city of Portland is a pretty perfect way to spend a summer evening. The staff is friendly and welcoming here, and the restaurant is informal.

The toot of the ferryboat might help you keep time. It's certainly easy to lose track of it here—part of the magical experience of Peaks Island.

Rockport
Samoset Resort and La Bella Vita

220 Warrenton Street, Rockport
Hotel: (207) 594-2511
Reservations: (800) 341-1650
www.samosetresort.com

La Bella Vita
220 Warrenton Street, Rockland
(207) 593-1529
www.samosetresort.com/la-bella-vita

Cuisine *ITALIAN* | Minutes from *PORTLAND: 105, BANGOR: 90*

*What comes to mind when you think about the Samoset Resort on the
ocean in Rockport? Luxurious rooms? Stunning ocean views? An awesome Italian restaurant? World-class golf course? A wonderful spa? Tons
of fun, with indoor and outdoor pools, hot tubs, saunas, workout rooms,
and classes? Well, this winter you should be thinking family school-
vacation adventures, romantic Valentine's Day experiences, and winter-
weekend getaways, packed with great food and fun!*

Samoset Resort

We love any excuse to visit the Samoset. On a
recent January weekend, our excuse was their
amazing ice bar. Amazing! It was a work of art
and packed with patrons, not at all discouraged by
frigid temperatures.

The Samoset's manager Connie Russell and
his staff are focused on the comfort and enjoyment
of their visitors. I always appreciate the little things they do for

us—extra K-cups for the coffeemaker and my newspaper in the morning, for example.

Our other excuse for visiting Rockland that weekend was the annual Pies on Parade fund-raiser for the local food bank, featuring thirty-five inns, restaurants, and businesses serving savory and sweet pies. OMG!

Room 423 at the Samoset now has our name on it.

Before opening my eyes on Saturday morning, I heard Linda say, "Oh! Wow!" She'd just raised the curtain to a stunning ocean view. I lifted my head slightly off the pillow and stared out over the water all the way to Vinalhaven, fifteen miles offshore. Wow, indeed! This corner room looks out at the Rockland breakwater and harbor from one set of windows, and out over the ocean toward the islands from another set of windows. The view just can't be beat.

The room has many amenities you'd expect from Ocean Properties hotels and resorts—elegance combined with comfort and convenience. I was especially impressed with the ergonomically designed desk chair.

Linda and I both love resorts where we can spend our entire visit without leaving the premises. At the Samoset, it's easy to do that, even in winter. They've got an indoor pool, hot tub, saunas, a health club, and many comfortable sitting areas—some with fireplaces and stunning ocean views. Their restaurant offers breakfast, lunch, and dinner, while their lounge provides another nice place to hang out and enjoy a beverage or a meal.

As we strolled around on Friday afternoon, making our plans for the weekend's activities, Linda noted a Saturday-morning hour-long workout called Building Strength and Power. Groan. She signed us up. We mustered out at 9:30 a.m. and were informed by a lady who entered the health club with us that it was a "great workout." Indeed. It turns out that playing volleyball once a week and walking four miles a couple times a week is not sufficient to keep me in shape. Holy cow! I thought I was going to die.

Saturday night, we enjoyed a lovely dinner at La Bella Vita, the Samoset's fine-dining restaurant. And then we fasted on Sunday morning to make room for all that food at Pies on Parade.

Daughter Rebekah and grandson Vishal drove over from their home in Union to spend Sunday morning with us and enjoy the facilities. Six-year-old Vishal is a swimming machine; actually, he's a boy in perpetual motion. He loved the hot tub, beat me in many swimming races, and then, just when it was time to leave, decided he wanted to hit the outdoor skating rink!

We didn't even get to the indoor kids' playroom, something the Samoset sets up for children on the weekends and school-vacation weeks. They've got everything from Ping-Pong to climbing stuff in there. Good thing Vishal didn't see that. We'd never have gotten to Pies on Parade!

The Samoset closed for a couple of winters, but thankfully, is now staying open year-round again, offering midwinter weekend getaways that will erase those cold-weather blues. We visited at the end of a weeklong stretch of sub-zero weather in January. We hadn't strayed too far from our woodstove at home all week, so it was great to head to Rockland for a change of scenery. And that it is! The panoramic ocean view from the corner room on the top floor let us appreciate Maine, no matter the temperature.

In fact, we'd come, in part, to see the "Frost" ice bar that had been erected out of eighteen thousand pounds of ice. We got our first glimpse of the bar, and all things ice, glittering like crystal just as the full moon was coming up over the ocean. Ice chairs and stools were draped with white fur; the chiseled tables and even a snowman ice sculpture had visitors snapping pictures. I felt like I'd been transported to Siberia.

The ice bar was crowded with all kinds of people, bundled up and ready to embrace the cold of Maine. What's that saying—"If you have lemons, make lemonade"? Well, if you have frigid, ice-cold weather, make an ice bar.

The following night we donned our warmest clothing for the ice bar experience. George started getting wimpy on me, saying we could get a drink outside and dash inside with it. I reminded him that we are from Maine and we could handle it. It looked like many people took George's approach as they huddled in the cozy inside bar. But we got a drink, sat on a large ice chair draped with fur, and enjoyed the spectacular moonlight dancing across the ocean.

While walking around the hotel Friday night we noticed a group fitness schedule by the health club area. We found out that all classes are open to guests and included in the resort fee. In the morning there would be a Building Strength and Power class. We were up for it.

Upon arrival, I met another woman and inquired if it was a beginners' class. "Oh, it's great; it's a really good workout," she replied. Well, that should have been a clue. We probably should have turned around at that point. I am a novice at exercise classes, and George has never been to one. The place was packed, and others guided us to retrieve the right equipment.

We did make it through an hour of full-throttle exercise (barely). At the very least, I'm sure we provided comic relief for everyone else, all of whom seemed to be regulars there. I was sure we'd feel powerful and strong as soon as our muscles stopped aching.

With special winter-weekend and school-vacation rates and activities, you should be thinking of the Samoset when those times come around. These getaways are packed with special family activities, culinary events, a kid's recreation center, the indoor pool—and don't forget the health club workouts! Our recommendation: Book a workout for the kids and spa treatments for yourselves!

La Bella Vita

Our late dinner on a frigid January evening at La Bella Vita, the Samoset's wonderful Italian restaurant, was a peaceful way to end a busy day. Tables are beautifully decorated with white linens and candlelight. From my seat in the upper tier of the restaurant, I could watch chefs preparing food and tossing pizza dough in the air in the beautiful **Enoteca Lounge**. We could also enjoy the live music of the saxophone and piano players in the Lounge. Lovely.

This is not a stuffy restaurant. You may order pizza, an array of cheeses, or a dinner. Our server, Ryan, pointed out specialties from each category, and thoughtfully informed us that the salad I was interested in was big enough for two. Thin fried onions sat atop a bed of mixed greens, salty olives, and gorgonzola. They'd split our salad in the kitchen, and it was still two good-size servings. Their reduced balsamic dressing made the salad perfect.

For the next course, primi selections come in large or small portions. We learned our lesson the last time we dined here, so this time we ordered two small plates of the fabulous pappardelle pasta. Last time I'd ordered the pappardelle and George had ordered something else, but he ended up grabbing most of my dish. So this time we each ordered our own. You really can't beat their homemade pasta and ragout of beef short ribs. The sauce is so delicious. My leftovers provided a lunch serving for both of us. A small serving was more than plenty!

Locals and visitors alike are taking advantage of the fact that La Bella Vita and the Enoteca Lounge are open year-round now. You will be delighted with the food here, any time of year.

There's something about candlelight, good music, and tasty Italian food, all enjoyed while gazing at a huge map of Tuscany, our favorite part of Italy. Looking at the map, I started planning our next trip!

The wine list is extensive. We selected a Chianti Classico from Rocca delle Macie, a winery we've visited in Italy. Maine diners are very friendly, and on this evening, we really enjoyed talking with a couple from southern Maine at the next table. They make an annual three-day winter visit to the Samoset, and love the resort and the restaurant.

Walking through the lounge to the restaurant, I overheard a patron say, "This pizza is amazing." While that comment was tempting, I stuck to my plan and ordered my favorite dish from our last visit, the pappardelle Farnese.

There are so many tantalizing dishes on the menu that we've got to break out of this pappardelle predilection next time!

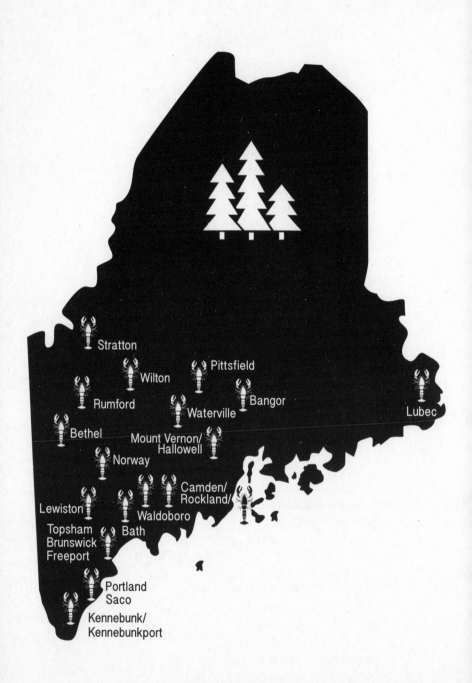

Stratton

Pittsfield

Wilton

Rumford

Bangor

Waterville

Lubec

Bethel

Mount Vernon/
Hallowell

Norway

Camden/
Rockland/

Lewiston

Waldoboro

Topsham
Brunswick
Freeport

Bath

Portland
Saco

Kennebunk/
Kennebunkport

Don't Miss
Restaurants

Bangor	11 Central
Bangor	Geaghan's Pub and Craft Brewery
Bath	Solo Bistro
Bethel	22 Broad Street
Brunswick	Richard's Restaurant
Camden	Long Grain
Freeport	Tuscan Brick Oven Bistro
Hallowell	The Liberal Cup Public House & Brewery
Kennebunk	Federal Jack's Restaurant & Brew Pub
Kennebunkport	Ocean Restaurant at the Cape Arundel Inn & Resort
Lewiston	DaVinci's Eatery
Lubec	Frank's Dockside & Takeout
Mount Vernon	The Olde Post Office Cafe
Norway	76 Pleasant Street
Pittsfield	Vittles Restaurant
Portland	Grace
Portland	Hot Suppa!
Portland	Zapoteca
Rockland	Café Miranda
Rockland	Rustica
Rumford	Brian's Bistro
Saco	The Run of the Mill Public House and Brewery
Stratton	The Coplin Dinner House
Topsham	Sea Dog Brewing Company
Waldoboro	Morse's Sauerkraut
Waterville	Amici's Cucina
Waterville	Buen Apetito
Waterville	18 Below
Wilton	Calzolaio Pasta Company

Don't Miss Restaurants

Most of us have restaurants that we always go to when we want to eat out. We had no more than a half-dozen—until we started writing our travel column.

We had no idea that Maine has so many fabulous restaurants! In the following pages, we will tell you about some of our favorites. Some we favor for lunch, and others for dinner. Some are inexpensive, and others, well, not so much. Please remember that some of our favorite restaurants are attached to our favorite inns and are profiled in the other sections of this book.

There have been many dining surprises since we started, including: the discovery of one of Maine's finest dining experiences in Stratton; astonishingly creative Thai food in a tiny Camden restaurant; German food in Brunswick better than any we have had in Germany; and New Orleans food in a small Portland restaurant rivaling the food we enjoyed in Louisiana destination.

And, oh sure, we'll direct to you to some very fine seafood. But Maine offers so much more!

Prices and hours of operation can change frequently, so we have not included them in the reviews in this book. Also, some places may close during the winter months. We have listed website addresses and telephone numbers and we encourage you use them to learn more information before planning to visit any of the places listed. We also encourage you to make reservations whenever possible, which can often make your travel experience more enjoyable.

Bangor
11 Central

11 Central Street, Bangor
(207) 922-5115
www.11centralbangor.com

Cuisine *AMERICAN* | Distance from *PORTLAND: 120 MINUTES, BANGOR: 0*

Gather Eat Be Merry, the slogan on our take-home bag from 11 Central, tells you all you need to know about this Bangor restaurant. It deserves kudos for its charming atmosphere, great service, and delectable food.

We began our evening at 11 Central in Bangor by meeting friends John and Julie Cashwell. Sitting at the bar for a pre-dinner drink allowed me to soak in the atmosphere. The restaurant has modern decor, but also features exposed brick and hardwood floors. The black tables are set with candlelight and fresh flowers.

Co-owner/manager Ann Marie Orr stopped for a chat at the beginning of our meal. She is full of energy, and you can hear the pride in her voice when she starts to tell us more about 11 Central. "Nothing is in here that hasn't been thought of with clear intention," says Ann Marie.

Once seated in the dining room we began our meal with bruschetta. John cautioned, "It is very large, just like the serving you saw at the bar." Thank goodness we listened, as there was plenty for the four of us! The crust of their bruschetta was pita bread, smeared with basil pesto and topped with lettuce, tomato, and black olives. Light, and so yummy!

Julie ordered the spinach salad, and I had a sample. Red and yellow peppers, locally raised bacon, and feta made this spinach salad the best I've ever had. Scrumptious.

Our entrees came with a wonderfully fresh Caesar salad. Ann Marie stopped by to encourage us to top our salads with a sprinkle of sea salt, set in a little bowl on the table, to "make the Caesar pop." Yup. Once delicious, now perfect.

I chose Chicken Oscar for my entrée, while everyone else went with fresh seafood. The chicken was lightly breaded, moist and tender. Two small cutlets were layered with lumps of fresh crabmeat and topped with hollandaise sauce. Rounding my meal was brown rice with roasted peppers and portobello mushrooms. What an incredible meal! It is one of their signature dishes.

As usual I said I didn't need dessert, and as usual, George asked what was offered. Our server Sarah said, "I have quite the spiel," and she did, whipping through a lengthy list of Ann Marie's desserts. At the end, she offered a funny head flip to announce the Shut Up and Kiss Me Pie. "You have to say this with the head motion," she said.

At that point I think we were all hooked, and John said we really must try it. I am always amazed that when I am presented with a dessert that is relatively light and contains chocolate—my appetite suddenly comes back! When I tasted the mint chocolate chip ice cream on a crisp chocolate crust and drizzled with chocolate sauce, I found my favorite dessert of the year!

 Details matter at 11 Central. The staff gathers every day before the restaurant opens to try the food, talk about the evening's service, "check attitudes," and decorate the take-home bags that bear the slogan: Gather * Eat * Be Merry.

From the seasonal art on the walls to the dishes to the speakers in the ceiling playing soft background music, everything is thoughtfully planned and presented.

Each server gets only three tables, so customers receive exceptional attention. We certainly kept Sarah busy for our two and a half hours at the table. We also spent an hour at the bar, nursing a glass of Angeline Reserve Pinot Noir wine from California and enjoying our conversation with the Cashwells. When Linda pointed out that it was ten p.m. and the restaurant was closing, I couldn't believe it!

As you would expect, the food was creatively exceptional. I loved the unusual presentation of bruschetta—enough for all four of us, although I probably ate more than my share, mostly because Linda and Julie were focused on the spinach salad.

When I asked Sarah for an entree recommendation she quickly responded with "the seafood marinara," describing it so vividly that I could not possibly order anything else. Fortunately, she did not overstate the case. It was loaded with sea scallops, shrimp, lobster claws, and mussels. The pasta—perfectly cooked—and the marinara sauce—with a nice spicy taste—are made here. The portion was humongous, and I had plenty left over for lunch the next day.

Bangor
Geaghan's Pub and Craft Brewery

570 Main Street, Bangor
(207) 945-3730
www.geaghans.com

Cuisine *AMERICAN* | Minutes from *PORTLAND: 120, BANGOR: 0*

While Portland grabs the headlines for foodies nationwide, Bangor's our kind of place, with savvy civic leaders, a great waterfront on the Penobscot River, events like the American Folk Festival, the new Cross Insurance Convention Center—and the awesome Geaghan's Pub.

 Bangor has a number of brewpubs, but Geaghan's is our favorite, with surprisingly creative food. You can get great beer now all over Maine, including at Geaghan's, so it's the food that keeps us coming back.

During the Folk Festival in August, we always eat one or two meals at Geaghan's, eventhough the festival features many good food vendors. After a hot afternoon at the festival one year, during which Linda made me dance to a salsa band until I swore I was going to require knee surgery, we hiked back to our air-conditioned hotel room for cold showers, rest, and dinner at Geaghan's Pub. Peter Geaghan gave us a tour of their new brewery, so popular that they've already added another tank a year ahead of schedule. They've got state-of-the-art technology and an award-winning brewmaster from San Diego. (He married a Maine girl who wanted to return home—lucky for us!)

Most of these exceptional beers are sold in the pub, but you can purchase them in both half and full growlers. Linda bought a half growler of Presque Isle Honey Blond Ale—a first for her!

My beer selection was Captain Kool, an IPA named for the nation's first female sea captain, a woman from Maine and a regular at Geaghan's until she died.

We sampled a fabulous white chicken chili (nicely spiced heat), and an appetizer we've enjoyed before: fried mushrooms. My BBQ Beef Brisket Sandwich sounded great and tasted even better. Brisket slow-cooked in their own Bangor Brown Ale, smothered in homemade barbecue sauce. Wow! What a meal! What a weekend!

We came to Bangor to enjoy the Folk Festival, so it was natural that we gravitated toward simple, easy food instead of a lengthy, lingering dinner.

We rarely drive by Geaghan's, no matter where we are headed in northern and eastern Maine. Each time I visit Geaghan's, I order Boneless Buffalo Wings. Their wings have become famous—even though they're not really wings at all. They're actually chicken tenders served with a choice of sauces (honey barbecue, honey mustard, or three levels of buffalo wing sauce). George gives me such a hard time because of course I always order these wings.

On our most recent visit, I learned some statistics that highlight the popularity of their wings. Sixty to seventy percent of Geaghan's takeout orders are boneless wings! Our server told us they have a very busy takeout business, especially on "game days." They sold five hundred pounds of Boneless Buffalo Wings on Super Bowl Sunday alone, and a total of fifty thousand pounds last year!

Somehow they have figured out how to bread and fry the chicken pieces without making them greasy, yet still keeping the meat moist. These are addictive, especially when eaten with the blue cheese dipping sauce and celery sticks. So even though their menu is full of great pub food, I plan on sticking with a proven winner.

We did try something new this time by sitting in the banquet room, which is open on very busy days and nights. With the Folk Festival going on, it was packed with a lively crowd. This room and the bar are our favorite places to sit.

For a late-night dessert we stopped back in to share a piece of Bailey's Irish Cream Pie. Made with a recipe that Larry Geaghan brought back from a trip to Ireland, this pie is decadent and unusual. Another thing I always plan to order here!

Bath
Solo Bistro

128 Front Street, Bath
(207) 443-3373
www.solobistro.com

Cuisine *AMERICAN / EUROPEAN* | Minutes from *PORTLAND: 40, BANGOR: 105*

Combine a guy who fell in love with food during a year of graduate school in France, with the globetrotting girl from Denmark he fell in love with, and what do you get? Solo Bistro in Bath—an outstanding restaurant with a European flair and very creative food.

Sometimes you can tell you are in for a creative dining experience just by the design of the silverware. Solo Bistro is one of those places. Modern and edgy is how I would describe the utensils and glassware. Angela Adams wall hangings accent the brick walls and are incredible pieces of art. And the modern lighting will grab your attention right off—big globes of rose-like swirls hanging from the tall ceiling.

Co-owner Pia Neilson grew up in Denmark and has drawn on her European background to design this space. The fact that this modern-feeling restaurant sits in the historic downtown of Bath makes it even more special.

We walked to dinner from The Inn at Bath with a light snow falling and a chill in the air. It was a beautiful walk as the snow piled up on the historic buildings.

Shortly after we arrived at Solo Bistro, a basket of freshly baked bread took the chill off nicely. For an appetizer, I ordered the baby arugula salad because it had a bit of a twist—it included feta cheese and spiced roasted chickpeas, which made this salad a standout. Wow!

My entree was a local mushroom ragout served over creamy polenta. It wasn't a vegetarian dish because they braised the mushrooms in duck broth, which lent the dish a nice richness. It felt like healthy comfort food with an amazing amount of flavor.

I've never loved kale when I've cooked it, but I certainly loved it at Solo Bistro. It was such a light meal that I could eat the whole thing and still enjoy all the bread and butter I wanted.

Solo Bistro makes their own sorbet and ice cream. My strawberry-raspberry sorbet held an intense berry flavor. FYI— it comes in three-scoop servings, so one serving would usually be enough to split.

I overheard the diner at the next table say, "This is like the perfect meal!" Well said.

In recent years we've received many recommendations for Solo Bistro. This restaurant draws foodies from throughout Maine, but Pia Neilson never loses focus on what the local folks want. I was impressed that the place was packed during a Saturday-night near blizzard.

While this is fine dining, the restaurant is not intimidating or dressy. It is superbly decorated, yet offers an atmosphere that is relaxed and comfortable. There are three rooms, one of which looks into the open kitchen.

At a nearby table, three generations of a family were celebrating a birthday. Many of them ordered burgers. That's right; this fine-dining establishment offers the "Bistro Burger." Boy, I'll tell you, if they'd been open the next day, Sunday, for lunch, we'd have gone back for those burgers.

The menu was impressive, and included: Moroccan spiced lamb stew and Grilled Faroe Island salmon. It was all I could do to pass over the seared duck breast that included duck confit cassoulet. While Linda was being good with her salad, I started with slow-roasted pork belly accompanied by a creamy polenta. The pork belly was thick and crispy yet tender, described by Linda as "like bacon, times ten." Sooo flavorful.

It had been quite a while since I'd had a steak and I was hankering for one, so I ordered the grilled New York strip with green peppercorn brandy sauce, herb-roasted potatoes, and sautéed green beans. The steak was incredible, perfectly seared with flavor packed in every bite. The sauce had a great zing. The green beans were cut into tiny pieces and were nice and crunchy. And the potatoes were tasty.

Portions are sizable here—another concession to the expectations of Mainers—but I still ordered a full dessert: ice cream with blood orange and mint. The chef also sent out a piece of walnut cake. As I dug in, my conscience (better known as my wife) said, "You're not going to eat all that cake and ice cream, are you?" It didn't really sound like a question.

Bethel
22 Broad Street

22 Broad Street, Bethel
(207) 824-3496
www.22broadstreet.com

Cuisine *ITALIAN* | Minutes from *PORTLAND: 100, BANGOR: 150*

Elegance combined with great food makes 22 Broad Street a must-see destination.

I still remember our amazing dining experience when we first visited 22 Broad Street in Bethel a few years ago. It was a perfect fall evening, and we dined in their charming screened-in porch. Tiny decorative white lights, intimate tables, a gentle breeze, and an extraordinary Italian meal remain in my mind.

So when we recently revisited the restaurant, it was great to see it still thriving. We visited this time in March, which ruled out the porch as a dining option. However, the interior of this historic house is cozy and elegant. A wood fire was blazing in the fireplace, flanked by decorative magnum bottles of wine and wineglasses, with a large bouquet of flowers and a mirror over the mantel. They have replicated the original tin ceilings and beautiful cornice that surround both small dining rooms. Nice lighting and braided rugs round out the peaceful atmosphere.

The chefs make the breads and desserts right here. How they get their rosemary focaccia bread so light and airy, I do not know. While George was having a second piece of our flatbread appetizer, I snuck a few more of the little focaccia slices.

The flatbread choices change daily here, and our version had capicola and pesto, along with the usual toppings of mozzarella and hot cherry pepper rings. The thin, crusty bread loaded with toppings is perfection, especially when dipped into their out-standing marinara sauce. "Holy mackerel," my hubby says after the first bite. I concur; it really is holy mackerel–worthy.

We split the green salad of baby arugula with deep fried gorgonzola balls the last time we visited, and I reminded George that we thought this salad was very special. Peppery arugula and grape tomatoes are tossed with fresh lemon juice and olive oil, but it's the warm fried gorgonzola that puts this one in a category of its own. It's both fresh and light.

One of the "House Favorites" (and "Smith Favorites") is the Crispy Eggplant Lasagna. Our server, Chuck, who has worked here for nine years and was friendly and helpful, tells us that although they change the menu here routinely, this dish always remains on the menu. On the first bite I remembered that this lasagna is one of a kind because there's no pasta in it. Layers of eggplant are fried, then layered with cheeses, marinara sauce, and roasted red peppers. The pasta comes as a side of rigatoni with marinara sauce.

I'd let George know that I was ordering the eggplant this time, and the only way I got around that was to promise him he could help himself to mine. The eggplant had a good dose of herbs and pepper—it's wonderfully different. The veggie side was a mix of broccoli, green beans, red peppers, and cauliflower cooked to crunchy perfection.

 We had visited 22 Broad Street a few years earlier and loved it. It's hard to imagine,, but I think it has gotten even better. Let's start with the dessert. When Chuck went through the list, which included "Frozen Moose," I wrote it down. Looking at my notes, Linda said, very wryly, "That mousse doesn't have two o's." Chuck got a kick out of that!

Alas, the frozen mousse was not yet frozen, so we ordered crème brûlee, a super-creamy standout. The charred taste of the brûlée'd sugar crust is so good. We loved this dessert because it isn't overly sweet. It was big enough to share (at least according to Linda).

The three dining rooms and bar were packed, but no one encouraged us to move along, and we lingered here for nearly three hours, watching an amazing array of dishes go by. Their selection of wine is superb, and, anything-Italy fans that we are, we selected a nice Italian Chianti, Santa Cristina Chianti Superiore 2013. The sommelier brought it to the proper temperature before serving it, a nice touch that you don't often see in restaurants.

I could have made a meal out of the flatbread appetizer. All the portions here are huge. Two folks at the next table ordered glasses of wine and appetizers, then had to apologize to their server when they were unable to order entrees. "I understand," said the server, very politely.

My entree was a special that night—scallops over linguine with artichoke hearts, asparagus, tomato, and cheese, in a delightful brandy cream sauce. It was good (and I had a lot of it left over).

While informal and comfortable, this restaurant delivers a very special experience, including your server cleaning the crumbs off the table after each course (okay, they were all in my vicinity).

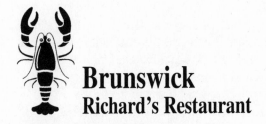

Brunswick
Richard's Restaurant

115 Maine Street, Brunswick
(207) 729-9673
www.richardsgermanamericancuisine.com

Cuisine *GERMAN* | Minutes from *PORTLAND: 30, BANGOR: 95*

Real German food makes Richard's a very popular restaurant.

Linda and I honeymooned in Germany, where I got hooked on German beer and food—and of course, on her. Actually, I was already hooked on her, and to her.

For years after that, I only drank German beer, until Maine's microbrewers took hold, and except for Morse's sauerkraut, I've not been able to find the German food I loved. Until now. I can't explain why we didn't get to Richard's a whole lot sooner—but I am certain we'll be eating there again soon.

Let's start with Richard Gnauck, a fascinating fellow who was the head chef at the famous **Harriet Beecher Stowe House** for fifteen years, initiating "German Night" every Friday, before opening his own German restaurant in Harpswell in 1988. In 1993, he bought a beautiful brick building on Brunswick's Maine Street and moved his restaurant. Richard's son Will now does the cooking, although Richard still likes to hang out and visiting with customers and help them with menu selections.

On the night of our visit, Richard had just returned from three months in Germany. We delighted in sharing stories of Germany with him. Almost immediately, he performed a miracle, convincing Linda to try a dark beer, something I'd been trying to do for a long time. "Dark does not always mean heavy," he told her. And she loved it! I chose the Weihenstephaner Korbinian, a double bock that was fantastic. If you are uncertain, try the sampler of four German beers.

When Richard told me he loves to eat liver, I told him our liver story. We were in Munich and had read about a nice restaurant in our guidebook where, as you entered, the room on the right (with white tablecloths) was for tourists, and the room on the left (with blue tablecloths) was for locals. We chose the room on the left, but couldn't read the menu. When we saw a gorgeous plate of food going by our table, we pointed to it and told our server that's what we wanted. It was liver, and we hated it!

Richard was a great help, recommending the Crepe Farci for an appetizer—crabmeat in a cheesy creamy sauce, inside a crepe. It was piping hot, nice and gooey, and the crab taste came through nicely. The portion was large, definitely enough for two people, although I ate most of it because Linda was anticipating a heavy entree.

I found it impossible to choose a single entree, so I selected the German Sampler, described as "a trip through Germany without leaving Maine." The dish included bratwurst, bauern-wurst, gulasch, sauerbraten, and both wiener-schnitzel and jaeger-schnitzel. It also included their German side dishes: Spaetzle (hand-pressed egg noodles), Klosse (bread dumpling), Heisser Kartoffelsalat (hot potato salad), Rot Kohl (red cabbage), and Weinkraut (sauerkraut).

Regular readers will be surprised to hear that I couldn't eat it all. I've loved German hot potato salad since I first tasted it, so I scoffed that up quickly. The red cabbage and sauerkraut were favorites as well, including all of the sausages. And the sauerbraten (pot roast) was fantastic.

Eliza, our server—and, as Richard described her, "Will's better half"—has worked here off and on since the late 1990s. Even when she lived out of town, she told us, she came back here to eat, calling the food "authentic." She got that right.

I was, for an hour and a half, transported back to Germany, sitting in one of their fabulous beer gardens, enjoying wonderful beer and amazingly tasty food.

Given the quality of the food, I was surprised by the reasonable prices. Richard explained that he is focused on keeping prices affordable, because he wants guests to come back next week, instead of waiting to visit once a month because of the cost. He's also proud that all of his staff has been here for five years or more. When he told me he sometimes teaches cooking at the Kitchen Emporium in Bath, I was tempted to sign up! But I could never cook food this good. Which is why I am so glad we finally got to Richard's Restaurant.

It was more than thirty-five years ago that we visited the beautiful country of Germany on our honeymoon. It was our first trip abroad, and we thoroughly enjoyed getting to know German food.

All of those memories rushed back with gusto when we visited Richard's in Brunswick.

Richard Gnauck came to cook at the Hofbrauhaus Restaurant in Ogunquit in 1968. His plan was to make a lot of money and return to Germany, but he fell in love with a girl from Brunswick, and he's still here—luckily for us!

We were able to chat with Richard, who still comes in to visit with customers even though his son Will is running the restaurant. His German accent is still detectable, and we found him animated and entertaining. We wanted a little guidance with the menu, and he was just the man to provide it.

I explained that I like a light beer, but he encouraged me to try Warsteiner Dunkel. He had a sample sent over, and I was pretty surprised to find that I actually enjoyed the taste of a dark beer. It was smooth and light-bodied without a hoppy taste. Richard explained that it had a "nice malt finish" (something I never would have been able to figure out on my own). So I ordered and enjoyed my first dark beer. George was thrilled.

I was hungry after a busy day with little food, so when the basket of pretzels and rolls came out, I dove in. Oh, those rolls! They were warm, flaky, and addictive.

I came knowing that I wanted sausage and sauerkraut. Richard suggested the Schlachtplatte. It included a grilled bratwurst (pork and veal), a steamed bauernwurst (German beef sausage), and a smoked pork chop (so good!). I couldn't possibly choose a favorite of the three, as they were all great. Their saltiness combined well with the side dishes I'd ordered. The Rot Kohl (red cabbage) dish was both sweet and spicy, while the sauerkraut and the hot potato salad were sour. And that's exactly why I love this style of food—there is no way on Earth one could describe it as bland!

Camden
Long Grain

31 Elm Street, Camden
(207) 236-9001
www.longgraincamden.blogspot.com

Cuisine *ASIAN* | Minutes from *PORTLAND: 95, BANGOR: 75*

The note at the top of Long Grain's menu, "Asian Home-Cooked & Street Foods," doesn't begin to describe the creative and delicious food in this very popular Camden eatery, our favorite place in Maine for Thai food.

Paula Paladawong's enthusiasm for the creative cuisine of her husband, Ravin Jakjaroen, had our mouths watering well before the food started to arrive. Paula is a vibrant presence in this tiny thirty-seat Elm Street restaurant. She told us about the local farms that supply much of the restaurant's meat and produce, and took us on a tour of the menu, which, honestly, was a complete mystery to me. Kimchi? Thai basils? Pad Seaw? Chiang Mai curry noodles?

By the time Paula had described each dish she wanted us to try, this meat-and-potatoes guy couldn't wait for them to arrive. Plus, the aroma of foods going by our table was making me very hungry.

Let's start, though, with the beer. For a small restaurant, the beer list is impressive, with choices from Vietnam, Japan, Thailand, the Philippines, China, Sri Lanka, Finland, Belgium, Scotland, Germany, and the United States. Paula recommended a Hitachino Red Rice beer from Japan, one of her most popular choices. I loved it. This beer had a nice ginger taste and was a refreshing match for some of the spicy dishes we tried.

I began my culinary adventure with a food I recognized: mussels. The broth was pleasingly spicy, not too hot, just right. I had Linda taste it, and she said the flavor came from lemongrass. They thoughtfully include a large dipping spoon with the dish, and I dipped liberally every time I took a steamed mussel out of a shell.

As the restaurant filled with people, I noted many younger diners. Linda explained that they are "more worldly and adventurous." I suspect she was comparing them to me. And she's right. So you unadventurous eaters need to know that Asian and Thai food need not be too spicy. There are plenty of tasty choices that won't set your mouth on fire.

Those choices would not include curry. But I encourage you to spice up your dining with the Beef Panang Curry with roasted red peppers, bamboo, and Thai basil. This was one of my favorites, very spicy indeed, with a large portion of beef that was soft and flaky and *oohhh* so good. But I must warn you: Don't eat the red peppers in the sauce! Paula warned me, but I managed to eat one, and it took the rest of my beer and a glass of water to douse the fire in my mouth. Of course, that was a good excuse for another Hitachino Red Rice beer!

 Long Grain restaurant in Camden features Thai food with a creative edge. Paula Paladawonga said they wanted to serve something a little more unusual than other Thai restaurants. Well, they've certainly achieved that goal.

Although there is an Asian influence to their food, they use locally obtained meat and produce as much as possible. It was fun to hear her excitedly explain the food on the menu. It's important to note that you'll get plenty of advice here to help you with your choices of dishes, ingredients, and spices. Many dishes offer a choice of meats, as well as vegan and gluten-free options. (Most dishes are put together in the kitchen, so ingredients can be changed to order.)

Four local organic farms grow vegetables for them, and some are trying to supply them in the winter with the use of greenhouses. They get their meats from the **Curtis Farm** in Warren. Long Grain strives for authenticity and home-cooked foods, making ingredients like kimchi and wide noodles right here.

The table was set with metal chopsticks, but don't panic. The server will ask you if you are okay with these or if you'd like silverware. "You'd better bring silverware for backup," George replied. And he never touched the chopsticks.

Each night Long Grain has a specials menu featuring in-season locally grown products. The daily menu is divided into appetizers, rice dishes, noodle dishes, stir fries, and a daily curry.

We welcomed some guidance from Paula. The garlic-chive rice-cake appetizer sounded intriguing, but I had to ask what a rice cake was. I was pretty sure it wasn't the dry snack food found in grocery stores. Sure enough, theirs is a light spongy cake which can be seasoned in a variety of ways. This appetizer was one of our favorite dishes of the evening. The soft texture inside the rice cake contrasted with the crispy pan-fried outside. They were served with fresh bean sprouts and a soy-based sauce. I have no idea what the spices were, but they were perfect!

We also sampled the rice cake in their highly recommended stir fry of house-made kimchi and rice cake. Their rice and noodle dishes offer a choice of pork belly, chicken, or tofu. We chose pork belly for our version. The kimchi surprised both of us. It is a vegetable condiment (mainly napa cabbage and carrots) fermented in a vinegary sauce full of spices that pack a wallop of flavor. The tang of the kimchi combines with the lean pork belly and rice cake to make an outstanding entree.

This dish intrigued me so much that I Googled kimchi when I got home. There are whole websites devoted to kimchi, as it is a famous Korean condiment. The best description I read claimed it was a dish that you have to get used to, but once you do, you will be hooked. I couldn't agree more.

Our last choice included their house-made wide rice noodles. Paula explained that it takes three days to make these. There is Pad Seaw, a mild version, and the spicier Pad Ke Mao. We ordered the spicier version, but found it was pleasantly mild. Wide noodles, thinly sliced pork belly, lots of Asian greens, mushrooms, and egg pancake pieces made a stir fry that offered very different flavors than either of the other two entrees.

Even though we were able to get smaller sampling portions of these dishes, we were full, with leftovers to bring home. We thought we were done, unable to eat another bite—until a serving of coconut custard brûlée came out for us to share. That first bite convinced me I had room for more! The serving of creamy custard came atop black sticky rice and was topped with coconut cream. What a surprise the sticky rice was—sweet and full of texture. This was absolutely delicious.

Long Grain served us grains in each course, appetizer through dessert. It sure would be easy to eat more grains, as healthy diets suggest, if I could make them taste this delicious.

Freeport
Tuscan Brick Oven Bistro

140 Main Street, Freeport
(207) 869-7200
www.tuscanbrickovenbistro.com

Cuisine *ITALIAN* | Minutes from *PORTLAND: 20, BANGOR: 100*

Great food and a beautiful restaurant, all within sight of L.L. Bean!

Going to **L.L. Bean** to shop for Christmas? Don't drive by the Tuscan Brick Oven Bistro, just north of Maine's most famous store! This restaurant is charming and beautiful, and the food is bountiful and delicious. This is a real find.

The interior—features lots of wood, including wonderful old wooden floors. I really liked the setup of tables, with a dining room to the right, separated from other dining tables and a long bar, and couches and comfy chairs along the windows in the front—giving you lots of choices. We were joined by our friends Ed and Cate Pineau of Vassalboro.

Our server Yvonne, a French native of Scotland, was very friendly and well informed. She was also very patient, explaining many of the dishes as we struggled to choose because of the many outstanding offerings.

Here's what I loved at the bistro: the brick-oven pizza, the Meatball-Stuffed Portobello, the Braised Local Rabbit, the Bolognese, and the Faroe Island Salmon. Okay, so those represent all the food the four of us ordered.

I'd been eyeing all the pizzas lined up on a counter waiting to go into one of the two brick ovens, and they looked delicious, so I was pleased when Ed ordered that night's special pizza. The piece he shared with me was great. It had a crispy crust of medium thickness, and was especially tasty topped with genoa salami.

I was even more grateful that Ed talked me into the rabbit dish. It was a slowly braised rabbit over hand-cut pappardelle pasta (my favorite—I love the thickness), with roasted sweet corn, sautéed zucchini, vine-ripe tomatoes, crimini mushrooms, and baby spinach, drenched in a delicious alfredo sauce and topped with smoked prosciutto crumble. There were even some bacon bits on top of that.

Portions are plentiful here, and I could only eat half of this. Luckily of the leftovers at home the next day made my lunch equally special!

Despite stiff resistance from Linda, I was able to order the meatball appetizer after promising to share it with all of them. And I did. It was absolutely delicious, and quite spicy—a veal meatball, wood-grilled portobello mushroom, San Marzano tomato sauce, Taleggio cheese, micro basil, and extra virgin olive oil. It has a distinctly smoky flavor, and was described by Linda as "not for the faint of heart."

They have a nice list of both wine and beer, including some of Maine's best brews. I enjoyed a generous pour of Nicodemi Terrana Montepulciano d'Abruzzo.

Linda had a glass of the Toscolo Chianti. It's tough to get her to order any other kind of wine, ever since our first trip to Italy. And trust me, we have a lot of Chianti at home!

Linda's Bolognese was fantastic, and my fork kept drifting her way for a taste. Cate also shared her salmon dish with me.

I love L.L. Bean, and now I have another great excuse to head for Freeport!

 First of all, most anything with "Tuscan" in its name is probably going to tempt me. It is so bad that when I last shopped for a car, I was immediately sold when told the car's color was Tuscan Red. So when friends Ed and Cate Pineau started tossing around the name Tuscan Bistro as a place to try, I was ready to go.

As I opened the impressive door to the restaurant I was enveloped in the smell of garlic, and I noticed a rooster on the menu—the unmistakable symbol of Tuscany. On our first trip to Italy, we were schooled to look for the rooster symbol on wine bottles, which signifies that the grapes were grown and the wine manufactured in the Chianti region of Tuscany. This is going to be a great meal, I thought, and indeed, I was impressed with every bite of food I tasted that evening.

George correctly assumed that I would want a glass of Chianti, and of course there were many nice Italian wine offerings.

My eyes lit up as our server Yvonne delivered two baskets, one containing Tuscan bread, and the other, black olive bread. As I dipped mine in some Italian olive oil, I decided this might be my idea of the best comfort food on Earth. I liked both, but it was the olive bread that hooked me. I went back for seconds (perhaps thirds), and wrapped the remaining two slices in the basket in a napkin to bring home.

I needed no more appetizer than the bread. Perfection. But I did try a bite of George's meatball-stuffed portobello mushroom. It looked like a meal all on its own, so it was lucky that we had four diners to tackle it.

Their menu offers a wide variety of choices, including brick-oven-baked pizza. The entrees range from risotto to many creative preparations of meat. Cate's Faroe Island Salmon dish was a beautiful presentation of fish, pilaf, and salad that included fennel and oranges.

I have to say that if a restaurant is making its own pasta, I'm pretty much sold on that section of the menu without giving the rest of it fair consideration. Narrowing down the type of pasta dish was an easy choice once Yvonne told us that their Bolognese was amazing, and very popular.

The Bolognese included braised beef from Pineland Farm and house fennel sausage in their version of ragout. The house-made trumpet-shaped pasta was cooked to perfection. The dish was topped with a dollop of fresh ricotta cheese, basil, and Parmigiano-Reggiano cheese. I fell in love on the first taste. That was the best ragout I have ever tasted, and that includes any I ate in Tuscany. I think it was the texture of the large pieces of braised beef that put it in a different class. I shared the dish with everyone at the table and it was unanimous—the Bolognese was off the charts.

The Tuscan Bistro focuses on obtaining local meats, fish, and produce, and has included a list of all the local sources of products they use on their menu. Attention to ingredients, presentation, and service make this a standout choice for lunch or dinner when visiting Freeport.

Hallowell
The Liberal Cup
Public House & Brewery

115 Water Street, Hallowell
(207) 623-2739
www.theliberalcup.com

Cuisine: *AMERICAN / ENGLISH* | Minutes from: *PORTLAND 60; BANGOR 75*

The popular hangout in the Capitol area has great food, and beer that is brewed on the premises.

At The Liberal Cup in Hallowell, there is a corner booth with a huge window that looks out at historic Hallowell's Main Street—this is my Augusta office. If someone asks to meet with me, it is this booth where I meet them for lunch. The Liberal Cup is located just a few minutes from the State Capitol, and many legislators, lobbyists, and others spend time here, for two good reasons: the beer and the food.

While I eat here often, I didn't get around to bringing Linda here until we started writing travel columns together in 2010. She immediately understood what I'd been raving about.

The Cup brews its own beer. They are a seven-barrel pub and offer a rotating selection of six taps plus a guest tap that features beer from another craft brewery. They brew their beer in small batches from twenty-six recipes. They also serve bottled beers. I favor their darker beers, including Tarbox Cream Stout and For Richer or Poorter, while Linda likes the lighter We All Scream Ale and Old Hallowell Ale IPA. Yes, we've sampled them all!

The Cup has tables and a bar in the entrance room, and a nice interior room with booths and tables. The Cup is busy for lunch, and at night it draws a crowd, thanks to weekly trivia nights and live musical performances. The restaurant was packed on the Friday night we visited, even though we arrived at 5:30. Still, we didn't have to wait long for a small table in the interior room.

I've never had a bad meal here—but admittedly I usually stick to the same lunch order and get the Cubano sandwich. (A Cubano is a variation on ham and cheese—but with the addition of pickles and marinated pork—that came to America from Cuba.)

However, for this dinner, I branched out, and was happy I did. For an appetizer, the chef sent us fried goat cheese and some fried clams—nicely battered and not overdone—with a super tartar sauce.

For an entree, I selected one of the night's specials, a whole roasted beef tenderloin wrapped in applewood-smoked bacon, and on the side, whipped potatoes topped with black truffle butter.

Owner Geoff Houghton says he fell in love with the idea of an English country pub when he was just seventeen-years-old. He started his career as a bartender in Damariscotta before opening The Liberal Cup in 2000. He describes an English pub as a place that is "cozy, informal, and meant for all to enjoy." The Liberal Cup is all of that. A decade after opening The Cup, he opened a restaurant and large brewery in Saco (the Run of the Mill Pub). So now you can see his beer on many menus throughout the state. Great news!

 Dinner at The Liberal Cup was a pleasure. The Cup's manager, Jess, was also our server, and provided good guidance—which you'll need, because the menu is extensive, and the dinner specials, particularly on weekends, are intriguing and creative.

The night we visited, choices ranged from pork to shrimp to steak to monkfish.

While the specials looked great, I ordered a regular menu entree, the Drunken Pot Roast, which was slow-roasted in The Cup's own brew. Trust me, this is not your mother's pot roast. Chunks of beef rest in the most delicious gravy I have ever tasted. With garlic smashed potatoes and squash, this is comfort food at its best. Other items on the regular menu include meatloaf, steak, Bangers & Smash, Home Style Turkey Dinner, and, of course, Fish & Chips. Our meal was served quickly—I don't know how they've organized the kitchen, but it's clearly a well-oiled machine!

For dessert, their cheesecake was tempting, as were four selections of berry pies, but we were nearly out of room. We shared the chocolate tiramisu, a delicious ending to a great meal. I made a mental note to accompany George to The Cup more often!

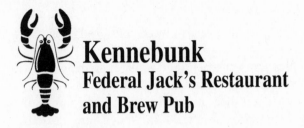

Kennebunk
Federal Jack's Restaurant and Brew Pub

8 Western Avenue, Kennebunk
(207) 967-4322
www.federaljacks.com

Cuisine *AMERICAN* | Minutes from *PORTLAND: 150, BANGOR: 40*

Great Beer, great food, and even a better location.

Shipyard Brewery's Export Ale is one of my favorite beers, and it was brewed first at Federal Jack's in Kennebunk in 1992. That history drew us to Federal Jack's Restaurant and Brew Pub for dinner in 2013, and Linda and I loved it.

So it wasn't a hard sell when I suggested that we host some of our kids and grandkids here during a visit in August. Joining us for lunch at Jack's were our son Josh, daughter-in-law Kelly, and new granddaughter Ada, along with our daughter Rebekah and grandsons Addison and Vishal. Josh once wrote a popular beer blog, so I felt like we were bringing along a real beer expert.

They say that location is critical for a business, and you couldn't get a better location for a restaurant. Federal Jack's, on the second story above the brewery, sits along the Kennebunk River looking across to Kennebunkport. You can walk back and forth between the towns over the nearby bridge, There are many shops on both sides of the river.

The view from the outside deck is stunning, which is why there was a forty-five-minute wait for a table there when we arrived. So we opted to sit inside. Actually, the views of the river from inside Jack's are nearly as good as those outside, and the air-conditioning made our visit more comfortable on a hot summer day.

We were even happier when our server, Neil, delivered ice-cold beers. The Goat Island Light was a table favorite. I went with Old Thumper, another favorite Shipyard brew. But in the restaurant, explained Josh, you get a different Thumper than I've been drinking at home. After his elaborate explanation, I gathered that this Thumper was brewed and served the "way English brews are supposed to be." It was actually quite different than my usual Thumper. Josh says that Shipyard's stouts and bitters—as well as many other Maine microbrews—are English-style beers. Made we want to visit England!

For our lunch, the array of food on the table was impressive. I had a grilled crab and Havarti sandwich, as did Kelly. Served on sourdough bread, it was chock-full of crabmeat, and the Havarti added a lot of flavor. The coleslaw was excellent, too.

Rebekah said her fish tacos were great. The pan-blackened cod was wrapped in flour tortillas with house salsa, fresh avocado, cherry-pepper-lime aioli, and shaved lettuce. It was served with a side of black bean rice.

Linda enjoyed a grilled chicken pesto sandwich with roasted red peppers, goat cheese, artichokes hearts, and greens on a roll. I tried a couple of bites and loved it.

Josh went with the Tavern Steak and Cheese, locally raised beef with American cheese and Thumpin' Onions on a soft sub rolls.

Addison and Vishal selected from an extensive kids' menu that offered everything from "Ants on a Log" to clam chowder. They even offered buttered pasta, which Vishal had with meatballs ("They know kids," said Linda). Addi had fish and chips, and I noticed that he put ketchup on his fish!

Josh, Kelly, and Ada live in Massachusetts. We took a ton of photos of Ada, imprinting our four-month-old granddaughter with the Maine coast. Earlier in the summer, Josh and Kelly took Ada to our North Woods camp, so she got a great early dose of Maine!

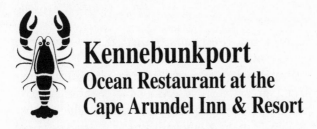

Kennebunkport
Ocean Restaurant at the
Cape Arundel Inn & Resort

208 Ocean Avenue, Kennebunkport
(207) 967-4015
www.capearundelinn.com/dining

Cuisine *AMERICAN / FRENCH* | Minutes from *PORTLAND: 45, BANGOR: 150*

The stunning ocean views are offered from your window at Ocean Restaurant in Kennebunkport's Cape Arundel Inn, but it's the food that is most amazing.

 You'd have to be on a ship to dine any closer than this to the sea. So of course, this restaurant in the Cape Arundel Inn is called Ocean. While the waves rolled toward us outside the huge picture windows, my gaze wandered to a side window that looks out in the direction of the nearby home of President George H. W. and Barbara Bush. They dine here, too, but not on the night we were there.

Actually, the drive along Ocean Avenue from the Grand Hotel, where we are ensconced for the weekend, is heavenly. And so is the food, served in a relatively small, intimate setting, a place of white linens, beautiful art, and superb service.

It's the first night here for our server, Piper, but she's already mastered the menu and is helpful as we make our choices. A cold glass of champagne kicks off the evening in style as we debate the list of ten small-plate tapas featuring mostly seafood, and more-substantial appetizers that include lobster thermidor and beef tartare.

I opt for sea scallops—not just because they are a personal favorite, but because the preparation sounded so interesting: parsnip brown-butter puree, shiitake mushrooms, Banyuls vinegar, and curry crisp. Piper said the curry crisp is a very thin sliver of baked parsnip.

The dish turned out to be just as interesting as described, different than any preparation of scallops I've ever had. The four small scallops came with a very tasty puree, while the mushrooms swam in the tart vinegar sauce. It was an enjoyable mix of flavors and textures, and the crispy baked parsnip flakes were really good.

The choice of entrees was equally challenging, ranging from Monkfish "Osso Buco" to Mallard Duck Magret. I was tempted by the mallard duck because I ate a lot of those during my duck-hunting days, and would have liked to see how the chef prepared it, but the filet mignon was calling my name.

For the record, the dish included seared duck foie gras, grain mustard sauce, pickled rhubarb, and roasted spring vegetables. I can't begin to adequately describe this for you, but the beef was tender, the asparagus and veggies crisp, the fingerling potatoes, delicious, and the dish, beautifully presented. Might be the best filet I have ever had, with a very rich, peppery taste.

We each enjoyed a glass of a French Bordeaux with dinner. We also noted a lot of cocktails going by to other tables, as well as champagne. Clearly this is a special place for celebrations. Three birthdays were celebrated there that night, and one group brought their own cake. We all joined in on the singing. Everyone was happy and delighted to be there—especially the Travelin' Maine(rs)!

Ocean provides a wonderful dining experience. As we drove from Kennebunk's Lower Village out to the oceanfront in Kennebunkport, I noticed the houses increased in size the farther we drove. Ocean is in quite a neighborhood!

The large restaurant takes full advantage of its breathtaking scenery. Its open dining room seems even larger because of its floor-to-ceiling windows. There are prime tables right at the front windows facing the ocean, but you can see the water from every table. Though it may be trendy to have dinner later in the evening, it would be a shame to miss the spectacular view while the sun is still shining.

Canadian-born chef Pierre Gignac worked in well-known Canadian restaurants before he opened 98 Provence in Ogunquit. It was a popular restaurant for eighteen years until it closed in 2012. So it is not only the view that draws diners here.

The spring menu was in full swing, with lots of seasonal vegetables and fresh seafood offerings. The asparagus salad quickly caught my attention as something truly creative. The dish was stunningly prepared with chilled asparagus spears that was topped with escarole lettuce, small cubes of prosciutto and Gruyère. It was accompanied by a poached egg and finished with an herbed-mustard vinaigrette. Perfectly toasted small croutons added a crunch. It was almost too pretty to eat. Almost.

My entree of roasted chicken had been rosemary-brined, making it supremely moist. Lattice-cut potatoes were not just a pretty side, they were super-crispy, lending a nice contrast to chicken. Cumin and honey carrots rounded out this great dish. Mmmm.

I had a bite of George's filet mignon, and it was extraordinary! Our memorable meal ended with us sharing (to George's dismay) the chocolate gateau. This was a warm, airy chocolate cake served with chocolate-ginger ice cream. I had to fight for my share of ice cream, and got little of the cake.

The restaurant was busy on a May night, and though there was lots of conversation, it was not loud. We began the evening in sunlight and ended it in candlelight, a leisurely two-and-a-half-hour dining experience.

Lewiston
DaVinci's Eatery

150 Mill Street, Lewiston
(207) 782-2088
www.davinciseatery.com

Cuisine *ITALIAN* | Minutes from *PORTLAND: 45, BANGOR: 100*

We've been enjoying Lewiston's DaVinci's Eatery for many years—usually before or after another great performance at the city's Public Theatre. We are generally there for lunch, so an October visit for dinner proved to be very special.

Lewiston's professional **Public Theatre** is an exceptional place to see contemporary plays and well as old favorites. Linda and I have been subscribers to the Theatre's annual series of four plays for eight years. For professional theater, this is a very good value.

At DaVinci's, we fell in love with "the rooster" (although we often opt for the half rooster). Their house wines are served in a ceramic Italian rooster pitcher that symbolizes good fortune. We feel lucky every time we walk into this place.

Our recent Saturday-night visit found the place packed, so we took a seat at the bar to wait for a table, enjoyed our drinks, and watched the food pass by. Lots of people eat at the bar and the tables in that area.

At their old quarters, DaVinci's had far less space, and we always had to wait for a table. The new space, in the Bates Mill Complex, is huge (300 seats, plus 80 in the banquet room), but broken up in ways that make the seating seem fairly intimate. The grandeur and features of the old mill, including the bricks, really stand out.

We were impressed that two of the restaurant's four managers, Stephanie and Laura, were on hand, along with a host, and all three spent some time with us, making us feel welcome. We didn't wait long for a table in the main part of the restaurant. The menu is as big as the restaurant, making it necessary to visit the restaurant many times to get a complete sense of their chefs' creativity.

A favorite entree of mine is Dirty Peas and Pasta. The dish includes Italian sausage, Bermuda onions, and peas sautéed and tossed in their homemade alfredo sauce, served over linguine. Really yummy. They even offer brick-oven pizzas and calzones, plus an interesting luncheon menu that includes a pizza buffet.

On this visit, I had the Pasta Bellissimo—scallops sautéed with mushrooms, broccoli, peas, roasted peppers, and onions, tossed with pesto cream sauce and served over linguine. Our server, Denise, talked me into it, instead of the sausage entree I'd decided to have. And I am so glad I took her advice. The scallops were not overcooked, the broccoli was crispy, the cream sauce was light. It was very tasty, and—like most of this restaurant's servings—huge.

They've recently expanded their menu and wine list, providing a nice selection of six white and six red wines in their rooster pitchers, plus a lengthy list of reasonably priced wines and a nifty group of more-expensive reserve wines.

For dessert, we opted for Gelato Fiasco's raspberry swirl and chocolate, a nice light finish to a great meal.

As George told you, we often eat here on a late Sunday afternoon. What a different place this is on a Saturday night! At seven p.m., people were waiting and still arriving.

The worst part of eating here is trying to choose an entree. The best part, while you're agonizing over the choice, is their garlic knots.

This time we tried their sausage-stuffed mushroom appetizer. The spicy sausage filling and light cheese topping make these great. A generous portion of seven mushrooms is enough to share. (I can't imagine one person eating all of this!) The sausage was so good (from **Maillot's Meat Market** in Lewiston) that I switched my entree choice to something with sausage!

Roasted peppers and fresh lemon make their Caesar salad sing. The dressing is super-light, not heavy like that of so many Caesars. The Sausage Milano, made with artichokes, capers, sun-dried tomatoes, and served with a butter wine sauce, was delicious. I could smell the garlic from my plate before I even tasted it, so I knew it would be great. It was so good that I enjoyed three more servings as leftovers just as much!

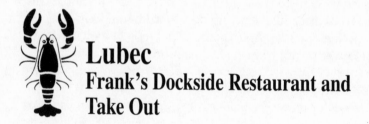

Lubec
Frank's Dockside Restaurant and Take Out

20 Water Street, Lubec
(207) 733-4484
www.franksdockside.net

Cuisine AMERICAN | Minutes from PORTLAND: 240, BANGOR: 135

Frank's Dockside Restaurant offers great food and scenic ocean views.

We love Frank's Dockside Restaurant and Take Out in Lubec for many reasons, including the awesome views of Cobscook Bay and Mullholland Point Lighthouse on Canada's Campobello Island. Chef Frank cooks in the smallest kitchen we've seen in a restaurant, while his wife, Wanda Corey, a

Lubec native, keeps the business flowing smoothly. We are thankful she brought Frank to Maine and opened this restaurant in 2010. And I just love that so many guests stop near the entrance to speak to Frank. He usually has something funny to say, no matter how busy he is.

For our dinner, Linda and I sat at one of the dozen inside tables next to a large picture window with a view of the bay. If we visit in August, the channel between Lubec and Campobello, just outside the restaurant, will be filled with seals. Very entertaining! Hanging on the wall just above our table was a photo of Wanda's Dad licking a bowl of fish chowder with these words: "It's ok to lick your plate." Frank's is my kind of place.

Frank's is a place that is dedicated to the town of Lubec—it's the only restaurant in town that stays open during the winter—and directs a portion of seafood sales to help finance a planned Lost Fishermen's Memorial.

Our personable and helpful twenty-year-old server, Kelsea, has worked here since she was fourteen. Her mom and her younger sister also work at Frank's—yes, it's a family-oriented place. Kelsea will attend the University of Maine at Machias and hopes to return to Lubec, where she is anchored and at home, to live after graduation. I loved the back of Kelsea's tee-shirt: "We rust before we burn out." Could be my slogan.

Frank is a creative chef and offers many specials. For dinner, I started off with crab-stuffed mushrooms, featuring crabmeat from our friend Priscilla Griffin who owns Griffin's Seafood in Edmunds. Her husband and son catch the crabs and cook them out back in a shed, and Priscilla picks them clean and sells them both at her house and to area restaurants. As I have mentioned before, whenever we drive to Lubec, we also always pick up a container of crabmeat from Priscilla. It is, quite simply, the freshest and best in Maine.

My entrée—Seafood Cobain—included shrimp, scallops, and more of Priscilla's crabmeat. The seafood was sautéed with spinach and topped with Cooper cheese, then baked. Yummy doesn't begin to describe it. Kelsea suggested I dip my crispy fries in the sauce—a great idea! And I got to lick the plate!

For dessert, we all enjoyed a double rainbow. Yes, a double rainbow appeared right outside of window. It ran right into the channel and up onto the lawn in front of us. Everyone – guests and staff—rushed outside to take photos. It was an amazing finish to a wonderful dinner.

 The food at Frank's is as spectacular as the view. When we stepped out of the car in the lower parking lot, I quickly noted that the deck, with eight tables, was packed even with a brisk breeze blowing. I thought—these people are hardy. On the other hand, the view of Campobello Bridge and the channel between Lubec and Campobello is worth a few goose bumps.

For an appetizer, I tried the Boneless Buffalo Chicken Wings. The small order provides a half-pound of wings and comes with Franks' housemate blue cheese dressing and celery. The Buffalo sauce has a nice kick of heat to it. I shared my wings with George, but we still had leftovers. (They were just as good reheated.)

The dinner menu features many tempting choices, including six styles of veal (veal is Frank's specialty) and many creative chicken dishes. A chalkboard in the restaurant is usually full of special appetizers and entrees. Our server, Kelsea, said that every dish is made using fresh ingredients; nothing is frozen. Frank loves what he does and cooks from his heart and you can taste it in his food.

For my meal, I ordered Eggplant Parmesan, which was described as "Delicate and Delightful." It was indeed delicate and delightful in taste. It included al dente pasta with Frank's famous red sauce. I couldn't eat the entire meal, but I did notice that I was not the only one with leftovers.

George mentioned the gorgeous double rainbow we saw after the meal. I am sure Frank can't promise such a beautiful sight after every meal, but he can promise great food.

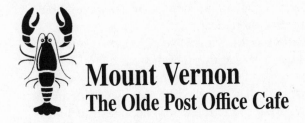

Mount Vernon
The Olde Post Office Cafe

366 Pond Road, Mount Vernon
(207) 293-4978

Cuisine *AMERICAN* | Minutes from *PORTLAND: 80, BANGOR: 80*

We love The Olde Post Office Cafe in our hometown of Mount Vernon for its lake view, featured art, and of course the food. We are excited that they now serve dinners Thursday through Saturday nights.

Whenever people want to meet with me, I ask them come to the cafe in downtown Mount Vernon for breakfast or lunch. And once they do, I don't have to ask a second time. I'm besieged by callers asking, "Can we meet again for breakfast or lunch at The Olde Post Office Cafe?"

Many small rural towns have a cafe, but few have one of this quality. Locals fill the place year-round, but diners also come from all over Maine, and in the summer, the street is filled with out-of-state license plates. It has amazing food, at very low prices. My hunting buddy Harry Vanderweide and I include breakfast or lunch here any day we are out after turkeys or deer. The cafe is an important part of our hunting experience.

The burrito is hard to pass up at breakfast, and haddock chowder on Fridays and Saturdays cannot be missed. The menu always includes some local favorites, but I often order the specials. The pastries here are to die for. Chef/baker/manager Sarah Chaisson presents scrumptious scones, muffins, and desserts. When Harry and I have breakfast here, we each order a full breakfast and we split a morning pastry. (And no, Linda is not going to be pleased to hear this!)

Don't leave without buying a loaf of bread, a pie, or something else off the shelf near the door or from the refrigerated case. Whenever Linda leaves a note for me that says we need bread, it's a license to shop at the cafe that day. Of course, it's the most expensive bread in the world, because it includes breakfast or lunch!

I'm more than a little partial to our town of Mount Vernon, and it was an enormous boon to the town when the Post Office Cafe opened. I can't imagine a prettier place for lunch. Big windows look directly out over Minnehonk Lake to the tree-lined shore across the water. The day we recently dined here, a small group was ice-fishing on the lake, and before we left it had started to snow. It was the picturesque winter scene found in a typical rural Maine town.

Arriving a little before noon, several tables were already occupied, and I knew everyone in the restaurant. People don't feel rushed here, lingering over great food and conversation. The staff will make you feel more than welcome, and will be checking in on you.

The lunch menu features panini and a variety of other sandwiches, as well as quiche and baked goods. But if you've never tried the soup here, you are missing something. Each and every soup I've sampled here has been special. I tried a cup of the Tuscan bean soup—full of white beans and carrots, and just plain delicious. Bob really knows how to season soups without making them overly salty. I always look forward to the soup of the day.

We ordered a Cobb salad to share, and neither George nor Hilary, our daughter who had joined us to eat, could believe that I'd never had one. The freshest of ingredients made this one very delicious. All of my favorites were included—bacon, avocado, roasted turkey, and hard-boiled eggs atop mixed greens, tomatoes, and cucumbers.

Norway
76 Pleasant Street

76 Pleasant Street, Norway
(207) 744-9040
www.76pleasantstreet.com

Cuisine *AMERICAN* | Minutes from *PORTLAND: 65, BANGOR: 130*

We wondered if the hour-long drive on winding roads on the foggiest night of the year would be worth it. And yes, it sure was! Our dinner at 76 Pleasant Street was unquestionably one of our best of the year.

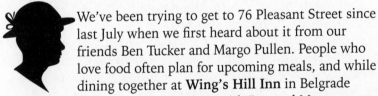

We've been trying to get to 76 Pleasant Street since last July when we first heard about it from our friends Ben Tucker and Margo Pullen. People who love food often plan for upcoming meals, and while dining together at **Wing's Hill Inn** in Belgrade Lakes last summer, we made plans with Ben and Margo to meet again in Norway. Six months later, we met at 76 Pleasant Street and enjoyed another spectacular meal.

The two restaurants are similar in that they are both old houses turned into intimate dining spaces where food is served. Owners Bret and Amy Baker offer two rooms for seating. Ours was full on a Saturday evening with the four of us, a table of six, and a table of two. The copper-topped tables look very elegant with candlelight on the table, joined by a big chandelier in the center of the room and a fire in the fireplace. The wall color, drapes, and artwork create an ambience you simply can't replicate in a larger restaurant.

There is a great variety in the food offered here. Starters include seafood chowder, three creative salads, flatbread, and heartier dishes of salmon gravlax, Moroccan lamb, and gnocchi. I ordered the roasted beet salad and now proclaim it the best I've ever had. What makes this version different is the variety of textures and tastes that sit atop the roasted beet chunks. Beautifully topped with mixed greens, it's the red cabbage ribbons, thinly sliced onions and scallions, fried leek strips, and curlicues of raw beet that set it apart. A small round of crusted warm goat cheese and the brandy vinaigrette complete this dish. It's a "celebration of winter" salad.

For my entree I selected the pink peppered filet of beef. Perfectly seasoned and perfectly cooked, the beef filet was tender. It was served with whipped cannellini beans and roasted mushrooms and garlic. The beef had fried ribbons of parsnips as a topping that added a wonderful crunch.

I noticed that the chef has included seasonal root vegetables in most of his dishes. They try to get local and seasonal food whenever possible. Margo didn't think she liked beets until she tasted my roasted beet salad.

Amy Baker is the face of 76 Pleasant Street. She has such a likable personality, you might feel as if you've known her for a while by the end of your meal. She effortlessly floats in and out, serving all of the guests. I noticed that she sweetly presented the young lady at a table of two with a piece of cake while singing "Happy Birthday!" Amy and Bret have been in the food business for forty years, yet this is the first restaurant that they have owned. They are naturals.

Built in 1896, this mansion comes with a delightful history, conveyed to us during dinner by Ben, a
native of the area. During a notorious 1938
murder trial, the jury was sequestered here—in
the judge's house!

Bret and Amy turned what had become a neglected duplex
into a stunning restaurant and home. They live here, and
deliver everything you could ask for in a dining experience,
from tasty and creative food to friendly and attentive service.
When all of that comes with very reasonable prices, you've got
a restaurant that will become a favorite of many—including us!

Ben told us that Amy and Bret opened the restaurant a few
years ago by inviting everyone in their Pleasant Street neighborhood to dinner, and they've anchored themselves in the
community ever since.

We followed Amy's recommendation with a bottle of Cam-
eron Hughes 2009 Meritage, a California wine. It was a nice
dry red that paired well with our food. They also offer one of
my favorite Maine microbrews, Cadillac Mountain Stout.

From the silver tray that the bread is served on to the beautiful drapes, everything about this dining experience is sophisticated. While they feature Maine produce and products as
much as possible, Amy and Bret don't hesitate to reach out for
the very best, including the bread (from California), which was
wonderfully crunchy and flavorful.

My starter of salmon gravlax included a delicious sauce,
pumpernickel, and caper berries. This was fantastic—including
the berries that I particularly loved. Appetizers are large and
easily serve two diners. In fact, we each had a piece of Margo's flatbread featuring prosciutto, fig, gorgonzola, and a port
reduction. Very tasty.

Having read a review of 76 Pleasant Street, I was deter-
mined to order the Charcoal Duck Breast. I did and it was to
die for. If asked to order my last meal, this might be it! The
perfectly-cooked duck was topped with dried fruit, coriander,

white pepper, and cinnamon, and accompanied by a Madeira demi-glace

I also tried Ben's porcini-dusted black cod, presented rare with a very flavorful sauce. The menu is limited to eight starters and eight entrees, plus specials.

Linda and I shared a crème brûlée for dessert, delivered in a heart-shaped dish. This seemed like the proper end to our dinner, because this restaurant really stole our hearts.

Pittsfield
Vittles Restaurant

107 Main Street, Pittsfield
(207) 487-8181
www.vittlesofpittsfield.com

Cuisine *AMERICAN* | Minutes from *PORTLAND: 90, BANGOR: 30*

Creativity and commitment to community make Vittles Restaurant special.

Vittles Restaurant is a family-run, family-style gem in downtown Pittsfield, just five minutes off Exit 150 on I-95. Bob and Kathy Phelan, the owners, are the parents of the talented and inspired chef Richard LeRose. LeRose focuses his creative energy on creating amazing dishes using quality, fresh, and preservative-free ingredients.

The restaurant is located in a building that is more than a century old with beautiful fourteen-foot high tin ceilings, as well as great artwork and decor. It has both tables and booths, plus a long bar for additional seating. Breakfast and lunch is served daily, but dinner is available only on Friday and Saturday nights and features a menu that changes every week. Most dishes are made from scratch and the restaurant strives for "farm to table" food preparation.

Bob wanted to start us with a specialty appetizers—Tempura Battered Garlic Scapes and Fried Calamari. We ordered half portions of each, and out came a rectangular plate heaped with curly garlic scapes, calamari, and fried jalapeño.

Chef Richard told us that he buys a lot of his fresh produce from Moodytown Gardens, a six-acre farm in Palmyra owned by Jarret Haiss and Johanna Burdet. Hairs and Burdet moved their farm to its current location and began restoring the seventy-five acre property in 2013. Vittles features ingredients from this lovely farm in his appetizers and entrees. He told us that he got an acre's worth of garlic scapes from Moodytown! That's an amazing amount of scapes— most people would see that as a nightmare, but Richard thought it was pure heaven.

Our tempura scapes were delicate and crunchy with a very mild garlic flavor. These were drizzled with a honey Dijon mustard sauce. You get your money's worth here, as portions are large and prices are low. Incredible focaccia bread, baked fresh daily, is brought to your table nearly as soon as you sit down. That night, they were offering cheddar and chive bread. My, it was good! The fried jalapeños paired well with the calamari, and were served with a marinara dipping sauce.

Their soups are great. We sampled the steak, mushrooms, and ale soup, with melt-in-your-mouth beef and a creamy base. Wow!

For my main entree, I was torn between the Sweet Pea Pasta and the Chicken Picatta. I chose the chicken dish. But before it even arrived, the kitchen sent out a small taste of the pea and pappardelle pasta. It tasted like summer—sweet, creamy, and delectable.

My Chicken Picatta was lightly breaded and moist. The white wine sauce with lemon and fresh basil made this dish very special. Like most of the dishes, the serving size was ample, and

I took half of it home. That evening's veggie side was corn with red peppers and onions. It was sweet, crunchy, and super fresh. The thyme-roasted Yukon potato wedges were yummy as well.

And for dessert, Vittles makes their own ice creams, which is so smooth and creamy that it reminds me of gelato. A must-try!

 Richard LeRose is a fantastic chef, focused on fresh food—some of which he grows himself—and he changes the menu weekly, making each trip to Vittles an adventure. I'd drive there just for his focaccia (baked fresh daily). And, oh yeah, their wonderful ice cream.

Richard is blessed with great parents. His father, Bob, makes the ice cream. We ate chocolate toasted coconut almond ice cream and it was divine. Bob spends his time out front, visiting with all the guests. Despite a full-time job, Kathy (co-owner and wife of Bob) still manages to make time to bake the pastries.

If you need more than the promise of great homemade bread to entice you make the drive to Pittsfield, let me tell you about my delicious appetizer and entrée. As Linda said, we tried a variety of appetizers, and I loved them all, with the fried calamari standing as my favorite. They were nice and crispy, and the accompanying tomato sauce was great.

For my dinner, I was initially debating between a couple of dishes. The fresh Maine haddock, broiled with lemon, white wine, and butter, set my mouth watering, but the garlic pesto cornmeal crusted scallops were calling my name. However, I'd eaten lots of seafood lately and was hankering for a steak. So, I choose Richard's beef tenderloin with shaved Portobello mushrooms, which came topped with a tasty sauce. They gave me a steak knife, but it was so tender that I didn't need it. I also enjoyed the side of crunchy corn and fried potatoes.

Bob said the restaurant's business has increased every year, which is no surprise to Linda or me, given how wonderful it is. There are now four cooks assisting Richard in the kitchen. No wonder Richard had time to visit with us!

I love Boy and Kathy's backstory. The couple, both nurses, picked up a copy of Down East magazine while vacationing in Maine, and saw the old post-and-beam schoolhouse of their dreams on eleven acres in St. Albans. The bought the property and moved here, anxious to leave behind a hectic life of Connecticut. Kathy now supervises a hospice and health care facility in the area, while Bob works at the restaurant. Luckily for us, they also brought Richard and his wife, Erin, with them to Maine, purchased a building in downtown Pittsfield, and opened Vittles, a small-town restaurant that has a strong local following.

Portland
Grace

15 Chestnut Street, Portland
(207) 828-4422
www.restaurantgrace.com

Cuisine AMERICAN | Minutes from PORTLAND: 0, BANGOR: 115

What do you get when you combine a beautiful and historic Methodist church with delicious, creative food and superb service? Amazing Grace!

Church suppers here could not have been this good. Anne Verrill performed a miracle, turning her vision for this former Methodist church building, which is on the National Register of Historic Places, into a stunning restaurant. I told Anne that we are Methodists, and our churches are supposed to be small white buildings. I've never seen a Methodist church like this one, built in Gothic Revival style. Anne restored the stonework, saved the unusual grain-painted wooden pillars, and let the rest of the huge church shine—including gorgeous stained-glass windows imported from Florence, Italy, in the 1850s.

I could have sat at our two-person table in the balcony with a glass of wine for hours, enjoying the reverence of this special place. But there was food to eat!

Our server, David, has been working here since Anne opened the restaurant. His professionalism and knowledge of the menu, as well as the features of the church/restaurant, were superb. This is fine dining, including a complete change of silverware with each course, but David's presence was never intrusive; in fact, we enjoyed the opportunity to visit with him at several points during the evening.

Anne is a hands-on owner, serves as the restaurant's expediter, and actually delivered our appetizers, giving us a chance to visit with her and talk about her experience restoring the church and opening the restaurant. She is vivacious and readily available to all guests.

We decided to be brave and try new appetizers. I will forevermore be looking for veal sweetbreads on menus. They were delicious, and I would have loved to take home a gallon of the bacon-braised cabbage. Juniper berries added crunch, and the local cider and mustard glaze was *sooo* delicious.

David recommended the Gulf of Maine sea scallops. They were seared with a nice crust but moist inside, just the way I like them. The Chinese broccoli added taste and crunch, and the mung beans were good too. I tried to tell Linda this, but she said, "You're mumbling about your mung beans." Shouldn't talk with my mouth full!

The chef and staff give a lot of creative thought to everything on the plate. While the primary ingredients—in my case, the sweetbreads and scallops—were great, it was everything else on the plates that made the dishes extra special. Or, as Linda so aptly put it, "It's not just ho-hum fried scallops."

We enjoyed the presentation of our dessert, a cheesecake ice cream sundae, as much as the sundae itself, which was light and fluffy, with a delicious salted-caramel sauce. The spoons for the sundae were shaped like shovels, drawing this remark from Lin: "Appropriate for you, honey."

A unique dining experience awaits you at the former Chestnut Street Church. Its size and architecture, along with its renovation to a restaurant, have made Grace a place you must experience. It feels a little surreal as you enter. Parting the simple green curtains and stepping into the foyer just might take your breath away. The height, expanse, and beauty of this room are hard to describe.

The entrance gives way to a spacious host station, a massive round bar with seating, and an open kitchen. Dining areas on the right and left offer a variety of seating options. I noticed a pew with tables to the left and a couch and relaxed seating area to the right. The upper balconies on each side are dining areas as well, with traditional seating.

For the Christmas season, greenery and white lights decked out the balconies. I found myself gazing around the restaurant the entire evening, just trying to take in all the beauty. They've preserved the structural beauty of this historic church, from its high arched supports to the spectacular stained-glass windows. One definition of grace is "simple elegance," and that certainly defines this place.

But of course the restaurant has earned its reputation because of its food. The chef searches out local and sustainable products to create an outstanding dining experience. They employ the farm-to-table concept, and believe in using the whole animal when creating menu items.

Warm house-made anadama bread served with molasses butter is a great start to the meal. The menu offers a variety of unique starters and selections from the raw bar, in-house-prepared charcuterie, and cheese listings. I decided to be very adventurous and try the roasted bone marrow. You spread the meaty marrow, served in the split bone, onto crostini. It was a rich taste unlike anything I've ever tried before.

I always feel a little bad about ordering chicken at a nice restaurant because I cook it all the time at home, and there are always more interesting choices on the menu. The Gianome Farm Chicken sounded spectacular, however, so when our server David pointed out that it was one of the most popular entrees, I ordered it guilt-free. The chicken breast and small thigh arrived in a classy presentation with house-made chicken sausage, spaetzle, foraged mushrooms, and foie gras.

The components of the dishes here are not just sides on the plate. They raise the dish to another level. The meat was tender and moist, while the seasoned coating made it delectable. George sampled it as well and was in full agreement. It was a spectacular entree. I did have a few leftovers that I neglected to share with George the next day. Heavenly.

Portland
Hot Suppa

703 Congress Street, Portland
(207) 871-5005
www.hotsuppa.com

Cuisine: *SOUTHERN-INFLUENCED AMERICAN* | Minutes from: *PORTLAND 0, BANGOR 115*

Hot Suppa offers unique southern food in a colorful environment, located in the West End neighborhood of Portland.

Whenever someone wants to meet with me in the Portland area, I insist on getting together in my "Portland office," a corner booth by the window at Hot Suppa, located in an 1860 brick Victorian on the west end of Congress Street. Featuring high ceilings, brick walls, and original moldings, the unique character of the building provides a complementary setting for the American classics that dominate the menu.

The cozy dining area is inviting, with a small bar, booths along one wall, and three larger tables along the picture windows looking out on the street. A huge chalkboard on the back wall lists the day's specials and brews—they've always got a good list of Maine micro-brews.

For a recent lunch, I enjoyed an Oxbow ale while Linda drank an Allagash white. We'd spent the morning at the Maine Restaurant Association's Expo, where food tempted us at many booths. OK, it tempted me, but Linda insisted we not eat anything there, so I only got a few nibbles when she wasn't looking.

This was actually a good thing, because portions at Hot Suppa are large and the menu is interesting. It includes burgers, sandwiches, and salads as well as entrees like Nashville Hot Chicken, Shrimp & Grits, steak, and catfish. The restaurant serves breakfast and lunch items all day, and dinner five nights a week. There is on-street parking only, so plan ahead.

For our lunch, we started with a side order of fried green tomatoes, one of our favorite dishes at this southern hot spot. In fact, if I'm here without Linda, I am required to order the tomatoes to bring home to her.

My favorite lunch items are the BLT and Cubano, and Linda ordered the BLT on this visit, making my choice easy. The Cubano is a Cuban-style roast pork and ham sandwich made with Gruyere, brown mustard, and cornichion pickles, on toasted French bread. Yummy doesn't begin to describe it.

Both Mo Sabina, the chef, and his brother Alec, the manager, grew up in the area and have become friends of ours, and they spent quite a bit of time visiting with us that day. In 2004, these brothers took a tour of the country, "eating their way across American's finest diners, barbecue feasts, soul food joints, and fish fries." Their website says they went from one out-of-the-way eatery to the next seeking the simple perfection of everyday regional dishes served in places where original recipes were still made from scratch. Inspired by their cross-country tour, they opened Hot Suppa in 2006. On their website, they list their local vendors.

Meanwhile, Alec's significant other, Angela Ferrari, a Farmington native, has filled the walls with her stunning works of art, all for sale at very reasonable prices. It's a real pleasure to enjoy that art during your meal. I've had lunch with lots of people here, and they all became regular customers. You should too.

The first time I tasted Hot Suppa's fried green tomatoes I fell in love. They are double battered before they are fried, and the batter is well seasoned. Once cooked, the crusty outside combines perfectly with the soft tangy tomato inside. Their addictive remoulade—a sauce made with mayonnaise, capers, cilantro and a dash of hot sauce (with some other spice I can't quite figure out)—has me craving these often.

George has finally understood that when he goes to Portland and has lunch there, he is to bring home an order of fried green tomatoes for me! When I go there for lunch I lean toward the Fried Green Tomato BLT, which features pimento cheese, pecan smoked bacon, pickled red onion, all on locally baked sourdough, whole wheat, or marble rye.

If grits are on the specials menu, don't miss them! They're flavored with bacon and jalapenos, and are so light that they almost have the texture of a fluffy quiche. Served with eggs and an arugula salad, this dish is deliciously different. They serve breakfast (their corn beef hash is famous) and lunch all day. We've been here for all three meals and can tell you, they're all great.

The southern cooking influence really shows up on the dinner menu—from chicken and waffles and shrimp and grits, to oysters and pork belly with red beans and rice. Mo went to school in the south and fell in love with the food. And now he serves it right here in Maine!

Portland
Zapoteca

505 Fore Street, Portland
(207) 772-8242
www.zapotecarestaurant.com

Cuisine *MEXICAN / AMERICAN* | Minutes from *PORTLAND: 0, BANGOR: 115*

Zapotec was a pre-Columbian culture more than twenty-five hundred years ago. Portland's Zapoteca Restaurante Y Tequileria brings the culture to the modern age while retaining the strong connection to that region of Mexico, from its decorations, to its flavorful and creative Mexican food served with flair.

We had driven around the block a couple of times, looking for a parking place, when we noticed that Zapoteca offers a valet service. We stopped in front of the restaurant and our car was whisked away by a friendly valet for free. What a great idea!

Before we got seated, Steve—who was keeping everything flowing smoothly that night, while co-owners Tom Bard and his wife Shannon were in New Hampshire opening a new restaurant—grabbed our coats. This is real service, and it continued throughout the nearly three hours we dined there. While patrons jammed into the front room and bar, waiting for a table, no one rushed us to leave. And honestly, it took three hours to work through this feast.

Because the menu is so lengthy and unusual, we'd asked for an experienced server who could help us through the meal. Kelsey, a six-year veteran here who is finishing her education at the University of Southern Maine, was both knowledgeable and enthusiastic, with a great personality that made our experience very special.

We were nonplussed by the lengthy bar menu, until Kelsey helped us select a couple of outstanding margaritas. I had the popular habanero watermelon margarita, nicely spicy with fresh fruit and juices and silver tequila. All of the margaritas are shaken at your table, and ours went extremely well with our appetizers. All I can say about the guacamole is holy moly! I would have bought a gallon to go. The chefs sent out two delicious tacos that are not on the dinner menu. And our Tres Sopes, a "tasting of three golden masa bites," could easily be a meal.

While I am embarrassed to admit how much I ate, I also ordered another appetizer—fresh halibut marinated in tangy lime juice with tomato, jalapeno, manzanilla olives, and avocado. It came with fresh tortilla chips and was just divine. Three ceviche appetizers offer choices of white fish, shrimp and calamari, and lobster. In my defense, I ordered a small portion. It usually comes in a much larger glass.

Steve insisted at this point that I try a flight of three tequilas, served with homemade sangria. Each was a half-shot, but they were powerful, and I sipped all three, then settled on my favorite, Gran Centenario Reposado, distilled from ten-year-old blue agave plants and aged in new oak barrels. Very smooth. The Bard's partner, Sergio Ramos from Guadalajara, Jalisco, Mexico, is an international tequila expert, and the restaurant features more than seventy-five of Sergio's picks.

We'd probably been there for an hour and a half by this time, having tons of fun. Kelsey and Steve constantly checked to see that we were doing well. When it came time to order an entree, once again Kelsey came through. We knew we wanted an enchilada, and we ordered the one with Maine shrimp. We didn't know that we also wanted the Carnitas de Puerco, a dish featuring braised pork, slow-cooked all night. Trust me—we will be ordering this every time we dine here. I was especially pleased to hear that the pork is even served as a breakfast dish!

While we decided long ago that we did not like most Mexican beers, Kelsey changed our minds with Pacifica (Lin) and Bohemia (me), enjoyed with our entrees. When sous chef Matt Burns came out to visit, we had a great conversation, including the wonders of a wood-fired oven—something that was already in the building when the Bards purchased it. Linda and I are big fans of wood-fired ovens.

Our leftovers were boxed and ready to go, but the chefs had one more surprise for us—a dessert to die for. When sous chef Scott delivered it, my mouth fell open. Ready and waiting!

The dessert is not on the menu, so I don't even dare tell you about it. But I will disclose that the sweet-corn ice cream, made by Joy, the restaurant's pastry chef who commutes by boat from her home on Peaks Island, was the key ingredient, and was absolutely phenomenal.

I can see why Zapoteca is so popular . . . Amazing food is being served. Their menu offers some creative dishes that are rare in Maine. It is Mexican fare, but not at all like your average Mexican restaurant. They make their own tortillas here; ditto for the tortilla chips. They make their own sauces, guacamole, and slow-braise their pork.

I had perused the dinner menu online and mentioned to George that I wished tacos were served at dinner so I could try them. (Tacos are usually a lunch item.) We had no sooner sat down than the chef sent out two creative vegetable tacos for us to try. He read my mind!

The tacos included Brussels sprouts and eggplant sautéed in chipotle butter and topped with arugula. Whoa! They were full of flavor and pleasantly spicy (although, not for the faint of heart). I ordered the trio of sopes—corn dough shells with three different fillings. It gave us a good idea of the flavors on their menu, with a sampling of chicken mole (more than twenty-seven ingredients in that sauce!), chipotle pork, and a black bean and fried jalapeno. The soft, slightly thick masa shell was so good, and very different. It was a great appetizer to split, and actually would make a great meal on its own.

George insisted on trying a little of their guacamole, and I'm glad he did. It was perfect—super chunky, with jalapenos and topped with tomato and cilantro. Where do they get such perfect avocados?

One entree we tried was the crab and Maine shrimp enchilada. There's nothing bland about the food here. They roasted poblanos in the wood oven and mixed them with crema for the enchilada topping. It was delicious. I noticed that they didn't serve salsa on the side of their dishes. There is no need, because their flavors are so true. No need to embellish (or drown) perfection.

Steve, the manager that evening, told us his favorite dish on the menu was the pork carnitas. The chef starts by roasting the pork overnight in a slow oven. Then it is shredded and pressed together, cut into serving portions, and fired in the wood oven to obtain a crispy crust. (It's slightly spicy due to a chipotle rub on top.) Topped with a tomato chili sauce, it's served with pickled red onions and black beans, along with grilled house-made corn tortillas on the side. I don't know when I've tasted something so differently delicious. It was smoky from the wood oven, crispy on the outside, yet moist and tender at the same time. I will dream of this dish.

Rockland
Café Miranda

15 Oak Street, Rockland
(207) -594-2034
www.cafemiranda.com

Cuisine *ITALIAN / ECLECTIC* | Minutes from *PORTLAND: 95, BANGOR: 95*

The menu at Café Miranda is all over the map, with Italian, Thai, American, and Mexican influences. Try to get a seat at the counter to watch the talented chefs at work.

Some restaurants are so special that I often find myself thinking about their food. That's certainly true of Café Miranda in Rockland. I can close my eyes and almost see their fire-roasted greens. Seasonal greens, caramelized onions, and mushrooms are roasted in their wood-fired oven, then served with a balsamic drizzle and a chunk of feta cheese. You know a dish is great when even George gets excited about a vegetable appetizer.

There are other reasons to love Café Miranda. From the lengthy list of appetizers and small plates, to Italian dishes inspired by chef/owner Kerry Altiero's grandmother, to large plates with American, Thai, or Mexican influences. Chef Andrew has been cooking the last few times we visited, and we were happy to see him once again. Kerry doesn't cook here much now, but rest assured, he is still involved in the restaurant.

We were lucky to sit at the counter where we could watch Andrew masterfully prepare dishes for a packed house. I cannot imagine how he keeps everything straight. He combines the ingredients, tosses the dish into the massive wood-fired oven, check on it a few minutes later, tosses on some greens before another round in the oven, and voilà! Miranda Magic has occurred.

It was a given that we would split the Fire-Roasted Greens Delight, which comes in a huge bowl. Meanwhile, servings of Miranda's incredible focaccia bread arrive—the best focaccia anywhere. The charred parts of the bread give it a unique taste.

I was torn between the Veggie Wowie and the Gnu Thing, both curry-style dishes. There was also Chicken X, an entree with Mexican flair to consider. Somehow I landed on Eggplant Parmesan, an item not even on my list but in the cookbook. There's a whole section of the menu devoted to Italian dishes, many with house-made pasta. Thick slices of eggplant are roasted without breading and topped with basil, marinara, and cheese. They add kale or spinach for the last few minutes and finish it off with rigatoni. The lack of breading lets the roasted eggplant shine, and of course, the marinara and kale make the dish even more special.

 I got whiplash watching Andrew's cooking performance—and just what it is as he "plays" the wood oven like a fine instrument.

Watching him work left me exhausted—but could also be because I ate too much.

Kerry Altiero is one of our favorite chefs and her cafe only gets better and better. He is constantly expanding the menu—a menu that you have to see to believe. The list of beers alone is eighteen inches long!

Kerry gives his staff a lot of credit for the Miranda magic. "It's a spirit, and you can't mess with it," he says. "It's all about honesty, integrity, and performance. HIP."

Kerry installed the second wood-fired oven in Maine, and has taught other chefs how to use them. He takes pride in being cited as an "Environmental Leader" by Maine's Department of Environmental Protection. He offers gluten-free dishes, including pasta—emphasizing that it is "good gluten-free." Gluten-free beer is also served.

There are so many appetizers that you could probably eat a different one every day and still be trying new ones a month and a half later. That fact makes it hard to explain why we always order the fire-roasted greens. Well, it's incredibly tasty, that's why.

I do venture into new territory on entrees here, so I bounced from the list of Miranda-style entrees to the comfort foods, lingering over those in the section titled My Italian-American Grandma. You can even get burgers, hot dogs, and pizza—something for everyone, for sure.

We were enjoying a sip of wine after finishing our appetizer, watching the action in the kitchen, when I saw Andrew pull a steak dish out of the oven, set it on the counter behind him, and cover it in a mushroom sauce. I started drooling, glanced at Linda, and whispered, "Please God, let that be mine."

"I'll tell you what," she replied. "If that's yours, you'll have leftovers." But she was wrong!

Well, not exactly, because I couldn't eat the mountain of fries that came with the meal, but I ate every bit of the steak—all with a smile. And yes, I remembered to thank God—and Andrew—after the first bite! The texture and taste was amazing, from the crispy mushrooms to the cheese to the perfectly cooked, tender, and well-seasoned steak.

The Café is a farm-to-table restaurant with its own "Head-acre" farm in Owls Head, and the two dozen local farmers, brewers, fisheries, and food artisans that supply the cafe are listed on the menu. Just another great reason to eat here, early and often!

Rockland
Rustica

315 Main Street, Rockland
(207) 594-0015
www.rusticamaine.com

Cuisine *ITALIAN* | Minutes from *PORTLAND: 95, BANGOR: 90*

*One of our favorite Rockland restaurants is Rustica. Chef/owner John
Stowe is exceptionally creative, and takes us back to Italy every time
we visit. Rockland continues to call us back—and not just because our
daughter Rebekah, son-in-law Patrick, and grandsons Addison and
Vishal live nearby in Union (although that helps). Main Street is full of
interesting art galleries and stores featuring clothing, cooking supplies,
wine, toys, and more. The **Farnsworth Museum** always has something
of interest, and we love the public walkway along the shore. This amazing coastal community has wonderful inns and restaurants.*

While walking down Rockland's Main Street one day
several years ago, we noticed a great possibility for
lunch—Rustica. The sign said "Cucina Italiana." As I
perused the menu, which included intriguing salads,
paninis, and pizza, I knew we had to eat here.
We were immediately taken with the decor and the open
seating space, with lots of dark wood. The menu choices all
sounded great, but that particular day was chilly, so we ended
up trying soups and splitting a panini. We were sold.

The soup specials change each day, but frankly, every soup
I've ever tried has been great. On our most recent visit we
enjoyed potato fennel soup. Yummy! The paninis hold creative
ingredients—roasted pork, eggplant, artichoke, or sausage and
mushroom.

The pizzas looked delicious. They are not your corner-store cheese and pepperoni variety. Look for margarita, goat cheese, spinach and feta, or chicken and mushroom. Creative additions to these pies (grilled balsamic onions, roasted garlic, and wild mushroom) make them really special.

I've got to say, the roasted beet salad is spectacular. Our server, Bridget, told us on our recent visit that it was one of the more popular dishes, and rightly so. The salad includes warm baby artichokes and roasted beets, arugula, goat cheese and champagne vinaigrette. Holy cow!

We tried the salad special, a panzanella salad. Arugula, green olives, tomatoes, cucumbers, and fresh mozzarella were combined with grilled focaccia chunks and served with a balsamic dressing. Other panzanella salads I've tried hold soggy bread, but not this one. Perfect.

You can tell owner John Stowe loves what he does. He's as passionate a man as I've ever met when he talks about his food creations. He values fresh ingredients, and understands Italian cuisine. He told us that he makes fresh pasta twice a week.

We got to try a handmade pasta on most recent visit—basil Alfredo over fettuccine. This amazing dish included homemade sausage, portobello mushrooms, tomatoes, and spinach.

John, also the baker here, wanted us to try a sampling of his cannoli and tiramisu. George loves cannoli, as do I, and John's are delightful. I don't like cake ordinarily, but I loved the moist and delicious tiramisu.

We've visited Rustica three times so far for lunch, but will make a real effort to get there for dinner soon. The lunch menu is wonderful, but the dinner menu looks tempting.

Well, there isn't much more to say, is there? Perhaps you've already left the house and are headed for Rockland! If not, let me add a few thoughts. The atmosphere here is Old World, the service is friendly and fun, and the food, both Italian and Mediterranean is great. I love John's homemade sausage! Although the restaurant has 80 seats, John often serves upwards of 150 people for dinner, so get a reservation if your party includes five or more. He offers a good wine and beer selection—we enjoyed cold Allagash Whites with lemon on the hot July day we last visited.

If there are two of you, ask for table six in the window, where you can watch the world go by. Both rooms are charming, and there is also seating at the bar. John relies on local customers. "That's who I cook for," he told us. You should become one.

Rumford
Brian's Bistro

25 Hartford Street, Rumford
(207) 364-3300
www.brians-bistro.com

Cuisine *ITALIAN* | Minutes from *PORTLAND: 125, BANGOR: 95*

A surprisingly fine restaurant in downtown Rumford, the place local folks dine—a lot!

The beauty of this space hits you immediately. The tall ceilings painted in black and accented with wide beams painted white are sure to grab your attention. The big open room with large windows and gorgeous old wooden floors has been artfully decorated by Jessica, who owns the Bistro with her husband Brian. She has a degree in design, which she has put to good use. I fell in love with the candle collections hanging in the front windows. Those candles combined with soft lighting make this restaurant more intimate.

George pointed out a beautiful painting he'd noticed while taking photos. It took up most of one wall. He asked Jess if it was Italy, and she said, "Yes, and I painted that." We were impressed! Not only is Jess talented, but she also has an upbeat personality. You can see that she's made many connections with her patrons, as they seek her out when they enter, or to say good-bye before they leave.

Brian's food has an Italian influence. He's a graduate of the New England Culinary School and a fabulous chef. We were going to pass up an appetizer, but Brian sent out an order of Risotto Rounds. I'm so glad we didn't miss those! These were asiago-stuffed risotto balls that came with the most delectable marinara sauce I have tasted in a while. I've tried risotto balls elsewhere that were huge and dry, but these little beauties oozed cheese when you cut into them. Yum! I inquired whether they used that same sauce on their pizzas. Yes, indeed. So those pizzas—seven very interesting combinations—must be incredible. They also offer eight styles of creative burgers. The burgers are so big, we noticed one guy cutting his in half before tackling it.

For entrees, choose from pasta styles (Puttanesca, alfredo, pesto, or gorgonzola), or Brian's chef specialties plates. That's where I found the Chicken Saltimbocca our server Kelly described as a customer favorite. I'd already spotted this dish while looking at the menu online, and thought that's what I'd order, but her recommendation sealed the deal.

Out came a gigantic plate of linguine topped with chicken, sautéed mushrooms, prosciutto, and sage in a Marsala cream sauce. The aroma that wafted up when it arrived was heavenly. It came out piping hot, and you could taste the Marsala without it making the dish too sweet. But it was the prosciutto that made this dish so well balanced. I ate and ate, shared some with George, and it still hadn't look like I'd even started.

Our meal was remarkable, and you can sense that this is just a happy place. Follow the signs off Route 2 to Brian's Bistro. You'll be very happy that you did!

The priest, the sheriff, and I were in the bar—that sounds like the start of a funny story, doesn't it? Well, it actually happened at Brian's Bistro. Because of the low lighting in the dining room, I'd taken my entree into the bar where there was more light, to take photos. Suddenly I heard the Oxford County sheriff call my name from a nearby table, where he was dining with the young local priest and the priest's parents. I visited with them for a while, promising that, with both a priest and a sheriff, I'd be on my best behavior!

The next time I went to the bar, two more couples spoke with me. And back at our table, two couples seated nearby visited with us and allowed me to photograph their entrees, as well. They also told us the Bistro's Caesar salad is the best salad they've ever had anywhere. Both the customers and staff were so friendly!

We love finding these community gathering places, many of which also offer surprisingly good food. Brian takes it to another level.

I'd been pleading with Linda for the Risotto Rounds as an appetizer, but the food police at my table pointed out that the entrees going past our table were huge, and we wouldn't be able to eat both an appetizer and an entree. Brian apparently read my mind because, even though we didn't order them, he sent them out! Wow, they were sooo good. As good as the rounds were, the marinara sauce was the star. I'd recommend anything on the menu with that sauce. Of course, when I told Linda I loved the cheese sauce, she explained that it's not a cheese sauce!

Our server, Kelly, a Bethel native, was excellent. Even though they were busy, she was always there when we needed her. While I'd been anticipating a steak dish, Kelly talked me into Scallops Provençale, pan-seared scallops topped with sautéed tomatoes, garlic, scallions, fresh herbs, and panko breadcrumbs. It was excellent.

The four perfectly-seared scallops were finished in the oven, nicely moist in the middle, and the sauce and toppings turned a good dish into a spectacular one.

I'd love to stop by here someday for a beer and pizza. The Little Italy pizza includes hot sausage, prosciutto, pepperoni, and bacon with marinara and mozzarella. Wow! That pizza is calling my name. Alas, Linda called it a "heart attack on a plate."

I had hoped for dessert, but Linda said "no." Imagine my gratitude when we got home and discovered that Jess had snuck into our take-home bag a delicious piece of chocolate-topped rum cake. You're the best Jess!

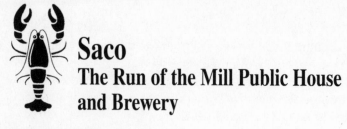

Saco
The Run of the Mill Public House and Brewery

100 Maine Street, Saco
(207) 571-9648
www.therunofthemill.net

Cuisine *AMERICAN* | Minutes from *PORTLAND: 20, BANGOR: 120*

Put the exceptional team at Hallowell's Liberal Cup into an old Maine mill with beautiful huge spaces, and invite them to create fabulous brewed-on-the-premises beer and tasty food, and what do you get? The Run of the Mill Public House and Brewery in Saco.

The Run of the Mill is anything but what its name suggests. Housed at Saco Island in one of the old mill buildings, I was not expecting the charming ambience of this sprawling restaurant. It's not big; it's huge. The massive bar and multiple separate dining spaces were all full on the Friday night we visited in April. And though they were extremely busy, an efficient staff kept things running smoothly. In the summer they open a large outside deck and offer a completely different menu.

The Run of the Mill feels cozy and welcoming despite its size. Extraordinary wooden beams, brick walls, and thick, hand-hewn tables are part of the decor. It was well-designed with smaller eating spaces to create a bit more intimate experience. The large "Mill" sign that hangs in the middle of our room helped remind me that this building had a very different purpose for many years, as a former textile mill.

With its own brewery, the restaurant offers many beer choices. Their lightest beer, Bug Lager, is very smooth, and one of the best I've tried. You will notice that they incorporate their beer into some of the food to create very tasty dishes.

Their Beer Cheese Soup varies each day, with different cheeses and beers. The soup the day we visited contained I Do ale plus asiago and sharp cheddar cheeses. It was just as great as it sounds. The creamy combination was so flavorful I started to think that perhaps I should have ordered a bowl instead of a cup. Served with pretzels on the side, this was an amazing starter.

The menu holds lots of options, and they offer many daily specials. All sounded intriguing, but lots of items on their menu are ones we've come to love at their sister restaurant, **The Liberal Cup** in Hallowell. Alas, despite all the options, I ordered an old Liberal Cup favorite, the Drunken Pot Roast entree. The beef is slow-roasted in their brew and served with spectacular gravy (no doubt due to the beer). A large portion of beef comes with garlic mashed potatoes and a perfectly sautéed mix of crunchy vegetables, all at a bargain price; in fact, prices here are very reasonable across the menu.

Their Mac & Beer Cheese, something George insisted on ordering, could make me into a mac and cheese fan. The topping of crackers and pretzels and the wheel of crispy baked cheese set this one apart from all others.

Imagine Hallowell's Liberal Cup with ten times more space, more beer and food choices, and a wonderful old mill location, and you'll understand why we were so delighted with our experience at Run of the Mill Pub.

Although we were there before the deck was opened for the season, I'm hoping we can return for the deck's opening-day pig roast, scheduled for a Sunday afternoon in May. That is, if Linda will allow it. This is an all-you-can-eat feast, and Linda doesn't usually let me near a feeding opportunity like that! The deck will be open on weekends after the pig roast until mid-June, when it's open all the time.

The pub's beers, all brewed right there, offer wonderfully diverse choices. I was happy to see the Mudflap Springbok still available, and it was superb. Later, I chose owner Geoff Houghton's creation, the I Do Ale, created for his wedding. Nice! Generous twenty-ounce "liberal cups" of brew are available (or sixteen-ounce pints, if the alcohol level is over 5 percent).

The menu that night included really interesting specials, from pan-roasted duck breast with rhubarb jam over risotto, to grilled hanger steak with roasted banana puree and barbecue-coffee crostini. But I opted for more-traditional pub food, starting with Mussels Dijon, something many online reviewers raved about. And they got it right. Sautéed with garlic, onions, red peppers, white wine, butter, and a touch of Dijon, these mussels were superb. I used all of the grilled baguettes that came with it to "sop up every last bit of the delicious sauce," as suggested on the menu.

Next up was the Mac & Beer Cheese with a triple-cheese sauce, cooked in Bug Lager, topped with crunchy pretzel crackers and Parmesan wheel, and served in a piping-hot skillet. No need to tell you how much I enjoyed this! Even the small portion was big enough for two of us to sample, and the leftovers reheated nicely the next day for lunch.

As I contemplated the creative specials for my next course, a plate of fish and chips passed by, and I was hooked. The plate included a massive hunk of fish, so I asked for a half-portion. The fish was fresh halibut (my favorite), and it was cooked perfectly, crunchy on the outside and soft and moist inside. And the homemade tartar sauce was delicious.

While the nine thousand people who once worked in these mills probably would never have imagined that all of their jobs would someday be gone, they would have loved the Run of the Mill Pub, and been happy to see their old workplace turned into such a wonderful, thriving restaurant and brewery.

Stratton
The Coplin Dinner House

8252 Carrabassett Road, Stratton
(207) 246-0016
www.coplindinnerhouse.com

Cuisine *AMERICAN* | Minutes from *PORTLAND: 150, BANGOR: 125*

The Coplin Dinner House offers elegance, creative food, exceptional wine, an extensive menu, and superb service that rivals restaurants in Portland.

Heidi Donovan and Tony Rossi have turned an old farmhouse into an amazing restaurant. Sitting in their comfortable chairs (secured from an old barn in New Hampshire), gazing out the window at Heidi's flowers, then turning my head to enjoy one of John Orcutt's photos on the wall while listening to Tony tell us about the food, I am in restaurant heaven.

Heidi and Tony are very personable, enthusiastic, and welcoming, and have put a great deal of thought into every detail of their restaurant, from the silverware to the layout of tables (Heidi gives the staff credit for this). There is a nice variety of seating, from a private space for a dozen guests, to tucked-away tables for couples, to the very popular bar in the back, to outside seating in the summer and fall.

Of the nine appetizers, I focused on the grilled Asian-style pork belly. "That's too filling; too much fat," Linda proclaimed. So I ended up with the fried Brussels sprouts. With the first bite, I forgot all about the pork belly. Probably because the dish included pancetta, which Linda kindly informed me "is meat— Italian bacon." No wonder I loved it! Actually, the candied pecans provided a nice crunch, and the sweet soy made this very tasty.

Since we visited in July, and Linda whips up wonderful salads every night from her garden, we passed on the four choices of salads and focused on entrees. This was a very tough decision. The dozen entrees all sounded terrific, from the rack of lamb and roast duckling to the red Thai curry, prosciutto-wrapped Cod, and hanger steak.

As we discussed each entree with Tony, when we got to the pan-seared North Atlantic halibut, we got into an extensive discussion about this fish, my favorite.

Halfway down the list of entrees, my eyes settled on the grilled meatloaf. Tony said it's a very popular dish—and indeed, we spied several plates of it going by our table to other guests. The pork comes from Tony and Heidi's own pigs. He adds some local ground beef and gorgonzola, and includes whipped potatoes and a mushroom demi-glace. Oh, oh, oh, I wanted it.

But I went with the advice of our server, Steve White (a guy who started his career at the nearby **Sugarloaf Mountain Ski Resort** in 1965, and is a very entertaining storyteller), and picked my second choice, shrimp Puttanesca. I now owe Steve big-time for his advice. It was very tasty, with capers, kalamata olives, aged Parmesan, and a red sauce over perfectly cooked fettuccine. Adding taste and crunch were lightly-cooked snow peas and a carrot. When Linda tried it, she figured it out immediately, exclaiming, "It tastes like Italy. All the flavors of Italy."

And then she looked up at me and said, "I think you have a piece of food on your cheek. It looks like a mole, and I know you don't have a mole there." It's helpful to have a wife who knows what you look like. And yes, the food was so delicious, I was wearing it.

The atmosphere is perfect—an old farmhouse renovated into intimate dining rooms, each set with white tablecloths and fresh flowers. Heidi has some vegetable and flower gardens growing, runs the bar at the restaurant, and has a young daughter. How she balances everything, I don't know, but her smile and ease with conversation makes her guests feel right at home.

Two cool summer soups were offered on the appetizer menu, one was local spring pea and mint. I found the chilled cup of fresh green pea puree held all kinds of flavor, accented with fresh mint. What a great combination! It was eye-rollingly good. The other soup was watermelon tomato basil. Now, there is no way in my mind that watermelon and tomato should work together, but believe me, it does. Tony had thickened the soup a bit with breadcrumbs to prevent it from being watery. The basil in this soup made it sing. I deem him a soup genius! Both soups came with a nice green salad with strawberries, and made a perfectly light starter.

Choosing an entree was a bit harder, but I settled on the Statler chicken breast. Steve told us it is a version of what used to be served on airlines. The moist chicken had a crispy exterior and was topped with an apricot glaze and goat cheese crumble. The sweetness of the fruit and the salty seasoning turned this into an outstanding chicken dish. With side servings of fluffy whipped potatoes and bright green snow peas, this entree was as pretty as it was yummy.

A couple with two young children was dining nearby. They were raising some very adventurous eaters. The kids tried the raw oysters and steamed edamame (fresh soybeans in the pod) just for the warm-up. I love seeing kids try new foods a try. The little girl declared the crème brûlée "the best thing I've ever eaten in my entire life!"

At one point, Heidi pointed out a deer walking toward us in the road. I thought it must've also been coming to dine from Heidi's garden.

I knew George was counting on dessert. He wanted the heaviest thing on the menu, a chocolate Bailey's brownie bread pudding with chocolate chip ice cream, but I convinced him to split the raspberry-peach cobbler instead. It was plenty big enough to share, and came with caramel-swirl ice cream. The hot and cold of the fruit and the ice cream along with the sweet and tart of the crumble and the fruit made a perfect balance.

Topsham
The Sea Dog Brewing Company

1 Bowdoin Mill Island, Topsham
(207) 725-0162
www.seadogbrewing.com

Cuisine *AMERICAN* | Minutes from *PORTLAND: 30, BANGOR: 95*

Don't be discouraged if the parking lot is nearly full; the restaurant is huge. And definitely eat on the deck if you can. Topsham's Sea Dog offers amazingly creative food—including a fantastic Sunday brunch.

The deck sits high above the rushing filled-to-the-banks river. A man in a red kayak floats in the eddy, casually casting to hoped-for fish. It's noontime, and the sun has just broken out, so welcome after a spring of days filled with drizzle and fog.

Inside, an array of food invites gluttony as our server sets mimosas down in front of us. When we arrived, a thick fog caused us to choose to sit inside, where a bank of windows offers views of the Androscoggin River. Later, when we walked out onto the deck, we wished we'd sat out there.

We'd heard good things about Sunday brunch at the Sea Dog brewery in Topsham, located in the old refurbished Bowdoin Mill, but when we finally got a chance to visit, every aspect of the experience exceeded our expectations. If you are leaving Topsham and driving over the bridge into Brunswick, you must have seen the old yellow brick mill. That's where the Sea Dog is located.

The atmosphere at the Sea Dog is cozy and relaxing. Though it seats many people, it's designed in such a way that you really don't notice just how big it is, unless you take a walk around the bar area. From our table, I noticed both kayakers and cormorants trying their luck at fishing. I know I won't be trying a kayak there; the currents and fast-moving water would scare me to death.

This brunch is impressive. One long string of tables holds breads and pastries, appetizers, and many offerings of hot entrees. In a U-shaped pattern the food continues. There's a great salad selection (loved their Caesar dressing), a carving station (serving lamb today), entrees cooked right in front of you, and made-to-order omelets. So my strategy was to try just a little of a lot of things.

One highlight was the chicken wings cooked in duck fat, as the sauce made them perfect. I was impressed with the Caprese salad, corned-beef hash, Swiss chard and cabbage, roasted garlic and asiago flatbread (wow), and Belgian waffle topped with blueberries, strawberries, and whipped cream. Although this was breakfast for us, we didn't try a cooked-to-order omelet or a couple other egg dishes—too many other great choices! Their crispy bacon puts the Sea Dog in my top-notch brunch category. The staff continuously checked that the offerings were fresh and in good supply, and our plates were whisked away by Kayla B., our attentive server.

I'm not a big cake fan, but I did spot a chocolate torte amid the many plates of desserts. Turns out it was the best of the dessert offerings for us that day. It also turns out that I got the last piece! Yes, I did share a couple bites with George.

For the purposes of these travel columns, I've had to alter my buffet strategy. Now I take small bites of lots of items, rather than feed like a pig at the trough. This turns out to be fun, although by the time I've sampled everything, there's no room for a large portion of my favorites.

While the Sea Dog would normally be a go-to place for beer and burgers—the "pub fare" I associate with brewery restaurants—we decided to do brunch here.

Favorite dishes included a fantastic spicy lamb stew (my overall favorite), Thai peanut salmon with black beans and rice (exceptional, with perfectly cooked salmon), corned-beef hash (always a favorite when it doesn't come from a can), biscuit with sausage gravy (too spicy for Lin, but I loved it—and shouldn't every breakfast include gravy?), potato salad with bacon, chilled Asian mussels, Caesar salad (you add the lemon and dressing), strawberry cream cheese crepes (delicate), dumpling with mango sauce (spicy), and roasted garlic and asiago flatbread (crispy and delicious—the only item that drew me back for more).

I know this sounds like a lot of food, but remember, I sampled. We'll be headed back to try a regular lunch soon. Next time, I'll enjoy my favorite Sea Dog Hazelnut Porter and the sun on my smiling face, while the river rushes by.

But Linda says no kayaks and no fishing gear.

Waldoboro
Morse's Sauerkraut

3856 Washington Road, North Waldoboro
(866) 832-5569, (207) 882-5569
www.morsessauerkraut.com

Cuisine *ITALIAN* | Minutes from *PORTLAND: 80, BANGOR: 80*

You can take a trip around the world at the Morse's Sauerkraut store in Waldoboro, but the real culinary tour is found in their small restaurant.

You've probably heard of Morse's Sauerkraut. The first kraut was produced in this old barn in 1918, and it's always been a popular product. The store draws people from a wide area, offering an astonishing array of products. They offer free samples throughout the store, so you can taste test many of their products. I particularly enjoyed the smoked whitefish salad (spread on crackers), and the cheese torta. Just to be sure, I sampled each a number of times.

But we were here to eat lunch in the Kraut House, opened in 2002 by Jacque Sawyer and David Swetman, two years after they purchased Morse's. The restaurant is tiny, and there's often a waiting line, especially in summer, but we lucked into a table just ten minutes after arriving.

Our server, Jen, was very helpful in explaining the menu, and quick to ask the chef to put together a sampling of appetizers for us. It was a plateful of delightful items.

I especially liked the Rotekraut, a classic German kraut of sweet-and-sour braised red cabbage with bacon, apples, and red currant jelly. It is served warm. But it was the Kraut Ball that stole my heart. Kraut Balls consist of Morse's sauerkraut, minced meats, cream cheese, onions, spices, and seasonings, all breaded and deep-fried and covered with a delicious onion-blossom horseradish dip. You may have had this dip before, but probably not with horseradish sauce, something distinctive to Morse's.

You will love the opportunity to mix and match things here. Choose your sausages. Choose your mustards. Choose your sauerkrauts. Choose your sides. Fun!

And speaking of sides, Aunt Lydia's Beet Relish with Horseradish is awesome—but have a cold drink handy. Linda asked how it was that I claimed to love this relish when my eyes squinted shut with every bite!

I had heard of Morse's Sauerkraut, but had no idea it was so steeped in tradition and had been in business since 1918. Once you enter the restaurant, housed in the original barn which once made all the sauerkraut, the old photos on the walls will help you understand the history behind this interesting company.

The store's two rooms are stuffed full of products to buy. You will find sauces, dips, mustards, a refrigerated section (with containers of their delicious sauerkraut), and an amazing deli featuring cheeses from all over the world. I was pleased to find queso fresco, after searching for it for two years.

There is a huge variety of Schaller & Weber top-of-the-line meats. I have never eaten such high-quality corned beef as that in my Reuben, and ended up ordering a pound to take home with my sauerkraut. The samples offered will tempt you into trying something new.

You'll find a vast array of European specialty foods offered here. If the restaurant is busy and you are waiting for a booth, this is a great place to spend time browsing. If you are in a hurry, you can order your meal while you wait for a table. The restaurant has only five booths inside and two tables outside. The staff is efficient and organized, and they often serve more than one hundred customers for lunch. That's a high turnover of tables!

On the large lunch menu you will find everything from appetizers to sandwiches to entrees and desserts. All of the sandwiches, including the huge Reuben, are served with pretzels, coleslaw, and a pickle.

What's all that stuff on the table? While you wait for your lunch, dig in to crocks of sour or half-sour pickles. Study up on the three mustards—whole-grain Dijon, sweet Bavarian, or hot German—so you can experiment by dipping pretzels or sausages into them.

When I think of sauerkraut, I think of two dishes: a Reuben, and a sausage and sauerkraut plate. Well, that's exactly what we went with.

Morse's fresh kraut, served cold, is unbelievably good. Their Haus Kraut is braised with onions, bacon, apples, and seasonings, and is served warm. We had this one on our Reuben. Mmmm. Classic German Rotekraut is a sweet-and-sour braised red cabbage kraut. It too was outstanding.

The Reuben served here is special inceed. It features marbled rye bread held a layer of tender corned beef, Morse's Haus Kraut, and onion-blossom horseradish sauce. It rates as the best traditional type of Reuben I've ever eaten. The large sandwich comes with perfectly crunchy coleslaw (they dress it lightly just before serving), a pretzel, and a Morse's pickle. One sandwich could easily feed two people.

Waterville
Amici's Cucina

137 Main Street, Waterville
(207) 861-4440
www.amiciscucina.com

Cuisine *ITALIAN* | Minutes from *PORTLAND: 75, BANGOR: 75*

At Amici's Cucina, we were transported to Tuscany.

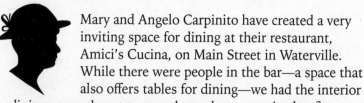

Mary and Angelo Carpinito have created a very inviting space for dining at their restaurant, Amici's Cucina, on Main Street in Waterville. While there were people in the bar—a space that also offers tables for dining—we had the interior dining room almost to ourselves when we arrived at five p.m. for an early dinner before a show at the **Waterville Opera House**.

Candles and nice lighting give this restaurant real charm, as does the Italian artwork, copper-topped tables, and background music. We were seated in a beautiful alcove by a window decorated with lights, white ribbons, and ornaments. It feels cozy here even though it's an open dining room.

Mary invited us to go out back to the kitchen to meet the staff. I was struck by two things—how sparkling clean it was, and its small size. The restaurant is pretty spacious, so I would have thought they'd need a big kitchen. Mary explained that everyone has their station and works well together. And they must, because the restaurant was full by six p.m., and the service was great. Five people staffed the kitchen due to the Opera House performance that evening. They are the only downtown restaurant that takes reservations, so they are busy on nights like this.

George ordered the sacchettis for an appetizer, a dish we both loved the last time we were here. This is a fresh pasta dish, little "beggar's purses" which hold a porcini mushroom filling. The deep flavor comes from the toppings—mushrooms, spinach, and cheese—and all this rests in a white wine sauce.

Angelo sent out a broccoli rabe appetizer that was on that evening's specials menu. I had never tried this vegetable before, but adored its slightly bitter flavor. The link of lean hot sausage served on the side made a great combination.

The warm bread with their seasoned olive oil arrived next, along with glasses of Cecchi's Chianti Classico. While sharing the appetizers I told George that this was plenty of dinner for me. I had forgotten that dinners here include a choice of salads or soup, and of course there was an entree course to come, too.

The Caesar salad was a nice size for us and left room so we could tackle our entrees. The house-made dressing on the salad had a nice lemon flavor. Fresh and delicious. George had anchovies on his and really enjoyed the salad.

Designer pastas are on the menu—choose your pasta, type of sauce, and a protein topping if you'd like—very tempting. There are American entrees too, if you must, including baked stuffed haddock, lobster, and steak, but I personally could never forgo one of their pasta specialties or Italian entrees. I ordered what was listed as the chef's choice of creamy risotto. That night the chef chose sausage (choice of hot or sweet), onions, and red peppers. Amazing. The rice was cooked to perfection and creamy. Why can't mine come out like that? It was a big serving, and okay, I will admit that I ate some for breakfast the next morning. Mmmm.

Lots of mmmm's were heard from both of us throughout the meal. The food here is fresh, served piping hot, and delectable. Take advantage of the fact they take reservations, make one, and head to Amici's for a memorable meal.

Chef Angelo is awesome. And sure, you can get steaks and seafood—the traditional meals served all over Maine, but I could dine here for weeks on end and always order from the designer and specialty pastas and the Italian entrees menus.

I'd already violated Linda's dictum that we only try new dishes this time when I ordered the sacchettis appetizer (fantastic), so I pored over the list of Italian dishes until my eyes settled on meat lasagna. I read, "Layers and layers of hamburger, sausage blend, and pepperoni with homemade marinara sauce and a wonderful blend of cheeses." Yes, yes, yes!

I later discovered that you can get the sacchettis with sausage as an entree, and that is now on my must-have list for our next visit.

Our server, Terri, could be called Terri Terrific, because she is very personable, knowledgeable, and was always there when we needed help, food, wine, or a good story. Her teenagers, daughter Tesla and son Devin, both work here, as does Mary's daughter and the daughter of the bartender. It's a real family enterprise.

I love the bread here, but at one point I heard Terri ask a group at a nearby table, which was ordering garlic bread, "Would you like that with or without bacon?" Perhaps I misunderstood, but bacon with garlic bread sure does sound intriguing!

The lasagna was wonderfully flavorful, and yes, it had layers and layers of hamburger, sausage blend, and pepperoni, with just-right homemade pasta. Truly yummy, and I was only able to eat half of it. I was staring at a beautiful painting, hoping for more appetite, when Terri arrived.

She arrived with a tray full of desserts. While Linda had emphasized, a bit earlier, that we would not have room for dessert, she cracked and allowed me to order a cannoli. It was crisp, sweet, and wonderful.

Waterville
Buen Apetito

4 Chaplin Street, Waterville,
www.buenapetitorestaurant.com
(207) 861-4649

Cuisine: *MEXICAN* | Minutes from: *PORTLAND 75; BANGOR 60*

We visit this popular Mexican restaurant frequently, and usually purchase their dipping sauces to bring home for our own Mexican-inspired feasts.

Buen Apetito is something I use to say often to my first grade pupils as they headed to lunch. It means "Enjoy your lunch!" (or at least, that's my translation). When you head to the restaurant Buen Apetito, it's a given that you will enjoy your lunch or dinner.

I admit I am addicted to their green sauce, which is served with fresh, crunchy tortilla chips (made on-site). I was under the impression the sauce was a tomatillo sauce, so in hopes of re-creating it, I actually planted tomatillos in my garden. I was wrong. Our server, Kim, explained that it's actually an avocado-based sauce. No wonder I love it so much! It also includes cilantro and chilies, and I could eat it on everything. Their chips and wonderful salsa are brought to your table as soon as you are seating, but a word of advice: don't fill up on them! Buen Apetito's guacamole outshines any other due to the chunky pieces of avocado, chopped onion, and tomato, as well lime juice.

For an appetizer, I ordered a serving of chicken flautas, which I have eaten during earlier visits as well. The appetizer features three flour tortillas that are stuffed with chicken and fried, served with lettuce, tomato, guacamole, and sour cream.

Three flautas came in each serving, and though some restaurants serve tiny flautas, Buen Apetito makes theirs large (it looked like there was an entire chicken tender in each one!). It was plenty to share. They were hearty and could be a meal on their own.

I'm afraid I can't sway from my favorite entree here. For me, the cheese chiles rellenos cannot be beat. I love the sauce and the topping of melted cheese. It comes surrounded by rice and beans on an oval plate. Poblano chilies are relatively mild, but the heat varies, and in this dish they certainly packed a punch. I enjoyed every bite, and I noticed George's fork often headed my way too.

Buen Apetito is Mexican food at its finest. George asked me why we don't come here more often. Great question!

Chef and owner Gary LaPlant also created a line of Deer Camp sauces several years ago. I serve his Buckshot Blueberry with pork tenderloin or grilled meats. His XXX Hot Sauce may seem intimidating, but a splash of it in chili, taco meat, or a stir-fry enhances the flavor without taking over the dish. However, my favorite sauce at the moment is Black Bear Bourbon Chipotle BBQ Sauce. The name is quite a mouthful, I admit, but it has a great balance of flavors, and it seems to go with most meats.

We began eating at Buen Apetito in the late 1990s, when it was in a tiny space across the street from it's present location next to the **Railroad Square Cinema**. In 2010, we first wrote about Buen Apetito. At the time you had to wait outside the restaurant in the theater's hallway, until a table was ready for you. For several years, chef Gary LaPlant, who owns the restaurant with his wife, Susan, said he was hoping to construct a bar/waiting area sometime in the future.

Well, he finally did it in 2015, adding a bar with ten seats and a waiting area with a few high tops and some seating for people waiting on busy nights. That is really good news, because every night is a busy night here. We often choose to eat in the bar area now, at a high top table.

Gary was able to more than double the size of the restaurant when he moved to this space in 2003. But it is still a small restaurant, with a very nice ambiance, and friendly servers.

I have many favorites here, but on this night I went wild and selected a special. Blame the handwritten sign in the waiting area that kept me staring at the BBQ Bourbon Beef Brisket. It featured four things I love! I chose to have it in a burrito, and I swear, it was a foot long, stuffed with meat, and sooo tasty.

"I can't believe anyone eats all this," I told our server.

"They don't, usually," she responded.

As I started to eat, I thought I might be up to the challenge, but the flautas appetizer ultimately made it impossible. Well, that and I very much wanted dessert. Gary's Mexican baked chocolate is something you'll dream about. With a mousse-like center and crisp top, it is served warm with vanilla ice cream. Ohhh my!

Waterville
18 Below

18 Silver Street, Waterville
(855) 242-1665
www.18belowrawbar.com

Cuisine *AMERICAN* | Minutes from *PORTLAND: 75, BANGOR: 55*

At Waterville's 18 Below, we loved the creative and tasty food, superb service, and gorgeous dining room.

The first thing you need to know is that 18 Below doesn't refer to the temperature. It's the location: 18 Silver Street in Waterville, below ground level (although if it happens to be 18 below outside, this is a very comfy place to spend some time).

When we started writing a travel column, we decided to give any new restaurant a couple of years before we visited. A lot can go wrong in a restaurant, and most of it goes wrong in the first year or two. But so many friends recommended 18 Below, we decided to set aside our policy and visit just fourteen months after it opened.

Owner Travis LaJoy's secret to success greeted us as we entered—his mother Donna! She's the vivacious host, and we thoroughly enjoyed visiting with her. She's obviously proud of her son and his restaurant. She handed us off to our server, Steven, who is knowledgeable, friendly, and eager to take the extra steps to make your meal memorable. I was especially impressed with the care Steven took in boxing up my leftovers, separating the broth from the mussels in my appetizer. You can plan on leftovers here, because portions are large.

Well, okay, I did eat all of my superb scallop entree. These were huge, caramelized scallops in a very tasty sweet pepper coulis. That sauce was delicious. And the scallops, cooked rare, came with two creative angel-hair pasta pancakes and seasonal vegetables.

Many online reviewers raved about the mussel appetizer, and they were right on. These Prince Edward Island mussels, sautéed in Shipyard Export Ale (one of my favorite brews), with shallots, garlic, tomatoes, and orange wedges, were exceptional. The sections of orange transformed the dish, adding surprising taste and zest. And the broth was very flavorful, too. I could have drunk a glass of it! Steve thoughtfully swapped my dish of empty mussel shells twice as I worked my way through the huge number of mussels—and I still had some to bring home.

I especially loved the walls of brick and old wood, the low lighting, the decorations—even the Allagash barrel that serves as the host station. Lots of thought went into the design of 18 Below. It's a compliment to say that this restaurant could be set down in Portland's Old Port and fit right in, offering high-quality food and a great dining experience.

The street-level lounge, called the Pearl, is gorgeous, resplendent in white, big enough for about two dozen people, and perfect for a small event. It has the same hours as the restaurant, and serves appetizers as well as drinks. The downstairs bar seats thirty-six, and is available for larger events. The restaurant seats forty-four. They don't take reservations, so be prepared to wait for a table on busy weekend evenings. Or go early or late. But definitely, go often!

 When you enter this restaurant, you'll probably notice the modern, edgy atmosphere. There is a large open waiting area in back of the host station where many patrons patiently wait for a table (on weekends), in the comfortable seating area. And I

can see why people wait—both the food and the atmosphere here are well worth it.

The menu features lots of fresh seafood, creatively prepared. There is a great variety on the regular menu, and a specials list includes five more entrees.

I ordered a tomato and fresh mozzarella bruschetta, which was one of the specials. The appetizer was very large, and certainly enough for two. Ciabatta bread was spread with an basil pesto and topped with fresh tomatoes and fresh mozzarella, which had been toasted just enough to melt it. All this was drizzled with a balsamic reduction. Served with mixed greens tossed with a lemon vinaigrette, this could have been my meal—absolutely delicious!

Although the pork tenderloin special sounded great, I stuck with a vegetarian theme and ordered the stuffed portobello mushroom entree. The stuffing was roasted tomatoes and spinach, and this was topped with parmesan cheese. The roasted flavor of both the tomatoes and the mushroom really came through. My dinner came with mashed potatoes and seasonal veggies, and was enough that I didn't make a very large dent in it. (It made yummy leftovers!) We noticed just about everyone that night exited with leftovers.

18 Below is a family endeavor. Mom is the host and Dad helped with the renovations. Son Travis is the owner who created his vision for the restaurant (with a lot of help from his wife), and helps with preparations in the kitchen.

Creativity and presentation are certainly strengths of the chef here. The variety of preparations combined with the wide range of proteins served here could have you coming back many times to try them all!

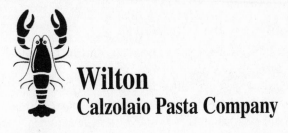

Wilton
Calzolaio Pasta Company

248 Main Street
Wilton, Maine
www.calzolaiopasta.com
(207) 645-9500

Cuisine: *ITALIAN* | Minutes from: *PORTLAND: 90; BANGOR: 100*

Tom and Rocell Marcellino offer traditional Italian favorites at very reasonable prices with great specials and friendly service to top it all off.

In 2008, we celebrated our thirtieth wedding anniversary at Calzolaio Pasta Company with a memorable meal, a wonderful bottle of wine, and a new diamond for Linda's finger. Since that special night, we've repeated the experience every year (well, without the new diamond).

On one recent anniversary visit, we began with a glass of the house Chianti for Linda and a glass of Montepulciano for me. We already knew that their salads are huge, so we decided to share a Caesar. We often order Roc's Eggplant Parmigiana, which is described as "a favorite of both Tom and Rocell's families." This baked dish features battered and fried eggplant layered with sauce and five cheeses. It's our anniversary dish and we both order it a lot!

But Calzolaio's is not just for celebrations—it is also great for a casual meal or a weekend lunch. This home-style Italian joint specializes in homemade sauces and pasta, brick oven-style pizza, fresh Maine seafood, and natural meats.

The setting alone is worth seeing. Calzolaio's is located in the historic G.H. Bass & Co. Shoe Factory on Wilson Stream in downtown Wilton. Bass opened its shoe factory in 1876 and by the 1920s, Bass shoes were a part of popular culture. Charles Lindberg wore Bass shoes on his transatlantic flight, Admiral Richard E. Byrd wore Bass ski boots during his first three Antarctic Expeditions, famed golfer Bobby Jones sported Bass shoes, and actor James Dean simply made them cool in the 1950s. However, in the late 1990s, Bass shuttered its Wilton mill and moved the manufacturing jobs to Puerto Rico and the Dominican Republic. It was a devastating blow to Wilton, a wonderful town of about 4,100 in the mountain and lakes region. A few years later, Bass closed all of its business operations in Maine.

Now Calzolaio has reclaimed some of that space and, in a nod to its historic location, displays Bass pictures and memorabilia on the brick walls of its main dining room. If you'd like to learn even more about G.H. Bass and the history of Wilton, you can visit **The Wilton Farm & Home Museum** located in the white building just at the head of the Calzolaio parking lot.

We love to bring friends to this historic restaurant. Our "special table" for anniversary visits is the main dining room in the corner, up against a beautiful brick wall. Among those we have taken are Tom and Shelley Doak of Readfield. This was Tom's first visit, but Shelley had eaten lunch there earlier in the year. We weren't surprised when our server, Rachel, recognized Shelley. If there is a more personable and professional server in a Maine restaurant, we have not met them.

Rachel not only remembers nearly everything Linda and I have ever eaten here in the past, but she is now comfortable making suggestions about what she thinks we should eat! While we initially wanted to share a salad on the night we visited with the Doaks, Rachel insisted we try the antipasto. We agreed and it was well worth it.

On our recent visit, Rachel had word of our arrival before we stepped through the door, and so she asked the chef to put cioppino, a seafood chowder, on the menu especially for us. Even though I had been looking forward to my usual eggplant parmigiana, I took Rachel's advice. I was so glad I did. I've eaten a lot of chowders and stews along the coast, but this presentation was perhaps the best. It was full of fresh mussels, clams, haddock, and baby shrimp, all in a delicious broth, and served with grilled crostini.

If you decided to bring friends to Calzolaio's, there is usually plenty of seating available. There are four eating areas, including the pub area, the main dining room, and the banquet room upstairs. In the summertime, weather permitting, there is also seating on an outside deck.

Dinner at Calzolaio Pasta Co. is consistently great, and I always look forward to an evening at the restaurant. Like George, my favorite dish is Roc's Eggplant Parmigiana. But on our recent visit, I decided to try something new. I had about dozen eggplants waiting to harvest at home and I had already been cooking many eggplant dishes, so I was ready for a different flavor.

Calzolaio gives me plenty to pick from. Regular entrees range from sirloin to veal to Maple Bourbon BBQ ribs, while signature entrees include Beer Battered Fish n' Chips, Smoked Salmon Alfredo, and Lobster Raviolo al Fresco. Both gluten free and take-out menus are available. I chose a dish off the vegetarian menu—porcini sacchetti. It featured two types of mushrooms sautéed with fresh vegetables, like zucchini, corn, and spinach. The vegetables were combined with pasta bundles filled with porcini mushrooms. It was topped with a rich marsala sauce, making it a lighter dish than if it came with cream sauce. Flavors popped with every bite.

When we told Rachel we planned to share a salad before our meal, she suggested we try the antipasto plate. What came out was an impressively large plate of sliced meats and cheeses, marinated mushrooms, black olives, tomatoes, marinated fresh artichokes, and roasted peppers. This beautiful presentation looks like it would fill you to the brim, but the dish is actually quite light. The thinly sliced meats and fresh or pickled vegetables wake up your taste buds. It's a wonderful display of fine Italian ingredients.

We love the ambience of the restaurant. And everything I've ever eaten here has been amazing—that's why we come back, time and again.

Safe Travels!

We hope you liked *Take it from ME*
and find time to enjoy the wonderful places
we have recommended. Please feel free to send
us any updates (georgesmithmaine@gmail.com)
to the information in our reviews or to let us know
about a great place you think we should visit. And if
you see us out and about please stop and say, "Hi."

All our best,
George and Linda